Karl Lage
biography

*The Man, The Myth and The
Extraordinary Life*

Note:

....

....

....

....

....

....

Herlind Gonzalez

TABLE OF CONTENTS

INTRODUCTION

As with any significant Chanel show, the situation was well known. On the stairs leading to the Grand Palais, young guys in black suits were receiving a briefing on their duties as stewards. Black limos double-parked on Avenue Winston Churchill are the cause of traffic bottlenecks. Women dressed in tweed lingered outside the massive Beaux-Arts structure, waiting to be photographed one last time before entering. On this final evening of spring, the sun is angling down on the glass palace, casting a gloomy light through the dome.

But on June 20, 2019, nothing remained the same in Paris. There was an empty place in the middle of all the frantic planning, the excited anticipation, and the vain displays. Four months after Karl Lagerfeld, the luminary of the bizarre parallel realm of fashion, passed away, his former followers had regrouped. His extended family as well as "Karl's family," as his closest friends and coworkers were usually referred to, came to say goodbye. Visitors from all over the world arrived, many of them wearing black, but others wore pink or white since they were aware that he disliked seeing people in mourning.

The official homage in Paris was dubbed "Karl For Ever." This was never going to be a standard tribute for a designer who liked not to linger on the past and even declined to attend family funerals. Instead, it was a wonderful evening of celebration that started with a procession of well-known figures, progressed via film homages, musical performances, and dancing interludes, and culminated in a champagne reception. This was the ideal tribute to a man who excelled at bringing people together as 2,500 people showed up in his honor.

In front of the Grand Palais, Le Tout-Paris halted. Among them were Carla Bruni-Sarkozy, a former first lady of France whose lengthy modeling career included a stint with Chanel, and France's First Lady Brigitte Macron, whom Lagerfeld had always liked because her husband, Emmanuel Macron, had succeeded François Hollande, not exactly his favorite French president. One of the fashion designer's closest pals, Princess Caroline of Monaco, wore a white shirt with a black silk bow. Charlotte, her daughter, joined her and she was dressed to the ankle in a black outfit. Inès de la Fressange, Claudia Schiffer, and Caroline de Maigret—former muses of Karl Lagerfeld—made their way down the glass palace's steps slowly to maintain their cool and avoid any awkward photos. The visibly touched model Gigi Hadid said to the cameras, "Whenever I visit the Grand Palais, I always feel like I'm going to see Karl. Today, I dressed as though I were getting ready to see him.

In his dying years, the guy who was closest to the fashion designer grinned enigmatically for the cameras. Former bodyguard, driver, and confidant of Lagerfeld, Sébastien Jondeau, arrived at the memorial dressed in a three-piece suit and shrouded by a cloak of mystery. Lagerfeld requested that his cremated remains be interred alongside those of his mother and his late life companion, Jacques de Bascher, who passed over thirty years before. Jondeau was in charge since he had transported Lagerfeld's remains to an unidentified place after they had been cremated at the Crématorium du Mont-Valérien in Nanterre. Just as he had intended, the fashion designer vanished into thin air.

Up to the 2019 couture show, when he was unable to attend due to illness, Karl Lagerfeld presented his universe in the Grand Palais four times annually. His two ready-to-wear lines each year as well as his two haute couture shows for spring/summer and autumn/winter were showcased in the palace, which was originally constructed for the 1900 Exposition Universelle. The show this time, however, was not focused on the upcoming season's trends. These two hours were entirely devoted to the life of one man, the various roles he had played over the course of eighty-five years, and the thoughts, words, deeds, and way of life he had led. Karl Lagerfeld was more than just a fashion designer, as was made abundantly obvious by the event's conclusion. He was also the creator of ideas, books, sketches, maxims, logos, phrases, careers, and ideals.

These images kept an eye on the high society affair in Paris that was put on by Chanel, Fendi, and the designer's own Karl Lagerfeld label. The tireless founder had dedicated his life to all three businesses and was now looking out over the caliber of elite spectacle he loved to see in person. It's possible that Bernard Arnault, who recently added Fendi to his LVMH empire—the largest luxury conglomerate in the world—has his sights set on acquiring the other two brands as well. However, on a night like this, France's richest man put aside business and struck up a nice discussion with Alain Wertheimer, who secretly controls Chanel with his brother Gérard. However, it's unlikely that the ravenous brand collector would have been happy with simple courtesies. The Wertheimer brothers may be losing interest in the prestigious brand now that they are both in their seventies and have worked in the luxury market for decades. After all, for the previous 35 years, Lagerfeld had directed the resurgence of Chanel. Now that he was gone, what would happen?

Karl Lagerfeld was not a very good father. The family he had created for himself was what was really important to him. Sébastien Jondeau said it best in one of the tribute videos that opera director Robert Carsen had put together, along with live performances, for this evening-long remembrance on the second-longest day of the year. "That was his strength: his ability to use the people around him and draw upon them for his creativity, for his own life and knowledge, to find out what was happening on the street," the Canadian actor said. According to Anna Wintour, editor-in-chief of Vogue, "He was the original multitasker, a man who did everything at once." Karl enjoyed social gatherings and people, but he guarded his privacy. He frequently expressed the desire to vanish after his death. That can't happen, obviously.

One of Lagerfeld's catchphrases was "no second option"; he made a commitment and followed through on it. This definite stance was as outmoded as his stand-up collar in an age of limitless alternatives, where limitless options lead to arbitrary decisions, notably in the fashion world. But his unwavering dedication was a real breath of fresh air, the antithesis of a culture where commitments dissolve and allegiances disintegrate. Karl Lagerfeld served as a living example of how to honor a promise and be true to oneself.

We travel all the way back to Lagerfeld's roots thanks to his distinctive rigidity and the rigid work ethic that never ceased to astound the French. Without his parents, sisters, friends, instructors, and classmates, it would be impossible to properly comprehend this man's life. Without the Prussian authorities, Hanseatic traders, and everyone else who came before him, this German's glittering career in Paris would never have come to be. Karl Lagerfeld's early life's facts have, up to this point, been mostly obscured by historical events, making it simple to overlook the real Karl Lagerfeld. The designer obscured his biography's traces in the tales he spun and the webs he spun, creating false leads for others attempting to learn more. Because so many of us are obsessed by our infatuation with this figure—who is simultaneously ageless and irrevocably connected to his position in history—and because journalists are all too willing to trust the portrait he built of himself, we have lost sight of the people who made him.

Chapter 1:
When he born (1933 to 1951)

On September 10, 1933, in Hamburg, Karl Lagerfeld was born. Given that Lagerfeld was never really pleased with this as his birthdate, this statement is far more complicated than it first appears to be. On September 10, 1898, Empress Elisabeth of Austria was killed in Geneva, he stated. Wolfgang Graf Berghe von Trips, a Formula One driver, perished in an accident on September 10. I detest looking back. Birthdays irritate me. The anniversary of the 9/11 tragedy was also approaching on September 10 too soon for comfort: "Am I really supposed to celebrate now, on the eve of this terrible date?"

Lagerfeld's birthdate and year were noteworthy historically for another reason: The pact, known as the Reichskonkordat, was negotiated between the Vatican and the newly-emerging Nazi Germany, and it was ratified by the German Reich on September 10, 1933. It was a significant occasion for Adolf Hitler, the new chancellor of the Reich and impending tyrant. The State-Church agreement between the German Reich and the Holy See gave the Nazi government, which had only recently come to power, a tremendous boost in "international credibility and legitimacy," in addition to enabling the regime to obtain the "approval of the German Catholics." The "führer" had so established his total control on the day Karl Lagerfeld was born, and in a few months, the government had "almost completely stripped away the principles of liberalism, democracy, and the rule of law." Everything happened really quickly. Federal elections were held on March 5 after the government was seized on January 30. On March 24, the Enabling Act gave Hitler the authority to pass legislation without the approval of parliament. According to the Führerprinzip, the dictatorship came into being quite quickly. By autumn 1933, "almost all the political and social institutions and organizations had either been brought into line with the new regime or outlawed" as a result of arrests, terror waves, and intimidation.

It was pure luck that this Sunday baby was given the name Karl. The most popular boy's names in 1933 in Germany, according to a reasonably representative study, were Hans, Günter (Günther), Horst, Carl (Karl), Werner, Gerhard, Heinz, Klaus (Claus), Helmut (Helmuth), and Walter (Walther). It is reasonable to say that developing a successful international career for oneself wouldn't have been as simple for a Günter, Horst, or Walter Lagerfeld. Karl Lagerfeld's success must have been aided by the fact that he possessed a distinct, monosyllabic, and universally identifiable first name to use for his public persona. Horst was a more overtly Nazi name, and Karl didn't require an umlaut like Günter. His best quotes are known as "Karlisms," and his political caricatures are known as "Karikaturen." Karleidoscope is a perfume from 2011, and the Karlito, a small talisman accessory by Fendi, also became a commercial success in 2014. It was also brief and snappy, lending itself to buzzwords that boosted self-promotion in later years. In the fall of 2019, Fendi also unveiled the Karligraphy bag. Over time, his conveniently catchy first name paid off.

This boy was the family's pride and delight even as a young child. Paul Sahner recalls the event as if he had been present: "The parents are overjoyed when godfather Conrad puts his thumb in the baby's palm to test his response. Karl Otto seizes the opportunity with vigor. In addition, Lagerfeld compared himself to a newborn, saying, "I slept well, had a huge appetite, and smiled at everyone." He once asserted that hearing the signals from the ships on the Elbe was his earliest memory. The pride of the family, however, was actually still a baby when the Lagerfelds left for the city in search of greener pastures.

Otto Lagerfeld's son Karl, who ate straight from the tin, was one of his biggest clients, and he lived right next door. Elisabeth, his mother, expressed her disinterest in nursing: "I didn't marry a dairy trader just to have to give up my breasts. Milk in cans is always an option, she noted. Little Karl was fed evaporated milk that his father's factory manufactured because his mother didn't want to "spoil her bosoms," as she put it. Fortunately, it didn't seem to hurt him.

In addition, Otto Lagerfeld, who was born on September 20, 1881, in Hamburg, owed a lot to evaporated milk. When he started the Glücksklee company, he was prepared for life, but only after serving his time as a young, aspirational merchant from Hamburg, traversing the world and putting himself in genuine risk. Otto Lagerfeld realized the true meaning of international trade while learning the trade's ins and outs and saw directly how world history might strike.

Otto Lagerfeld Sr., who was born in 1845, was also a businessman. The 1910 Hamburg telephone book lists his name along with the following description: "Wine shop and authorized wine importer, general warehouse of the Grande Chartreuse (Pères Chartreux in Tarragona)." In Hamburg's old town, near to the inland harbor, at 74 Rödingsmarkt, the booze merchant offered his foreign goods, including herbal liqueur. In the Ottensen area, at number 70 on the renowned Elbchaussee, which connects the Elbe suburbs with the district of Altona and the inner city, his son Otto built him a house for his old age. When Tönnies Johann Otto Lagerfeld passed away on June 22, 1931, at the age of 85, this was the address to send condolence messages. When his wife Maria Lagerfeld (née Wiegels) passed away on March 13, 1936, the residence with a view of the Elbe was also mentioned in her obituary. Back then, the entire Elbchaussee neighborhood—including the Ottensen end, where the Lagerfelds lived—was a much-desired residential neighborhood than it is now. Living in an even-numbered house on the right side of town on the way out was advantageous at the time because there weren't many cars around. These days, getting to the banks of the Elbe on the other side requires crossing a bustling thoroughfare.

Otto Lagerfeld Jr., one of eleven children, wanted to follow in his father's business career. He finished his apprenticeship with a Hamburg-based coffee exporter, was drafted into the military, and in late 1902, on assignment for the Hamburg firm Van Dissel, Rode & Co., moved to Maracaibo, Venezuela. Around this period, there was a great demand for Venezuelan coffee in Hamburg, but getting supply required risky travel. Otto was putting himself at risk of contracting the widespread yellow fever that was being spread by mosquitoes throughout the marshy landscape by accepting the assignment in Maracaibo. Due to the drop in coffee prices, he was also exposing himself to political turmoil in the area. When the Thousand Days' War broke out in Colombia in 1899 as a result of uprisings there, trade with the neighboring nation came to a complete halt. Work on the plantations became more and more challenging due to guerilla conflict. Then came the Venezuelan Crisis of 1902–1903, which was a naval blockade of the nation by Great Britain, Germany, and Italy that led to the detention of numerous German citizens.

Karl Lagerfeld observed that his father was aloof and distant. His mother was more accessible to him and constantly had something to say. This woman's candid remarks revealed not only her wicked sense of humor, but also an unyielding strictness and impossible standards. Elisabeth Lagerfeld didn't seem like the most maternal person with all the stories and harsh comments her son revealed to a shocked audience over the years. She predicted her lofty expectations onto her son without any restraint, which both irritated and inspired him at the same time.

Elisabeth's story must be examined closely if we are to understand her behavior. She was raised in the somewhat rural environment of this town between Münster and Paderborn in North Rhine-Westphalia, whose population was less than ten thousand at the start of the twentieth century. She was the daughter of the district administrator for Beckum. Elisabeth and her older sister, Felicitas Bahlmann, were raised in a mobile family and were aware of their roots being abroad. They also had a prominent position in this rural setting because their father was the district administrator, which made it simpler for them to break out of certain childhood habits than the kids of residents who had been in the town for a longer period of time.

Elisabeth was two years old when her family relocated to Beckum from her birthplace of Gammertingen in the Sigmaringen region of Baden-Württemberg. She must have felt like a princess, as did her older sister Felicitas. The Kreisständehaus building in Beckum housed them on the ground floor in a sizable official home. With its majestic proportions and expansive back gardens, the beautiful neo-Gothic structure from 1886 or 1887—now known as the Altes Kreishaus—was a child's dream come true. The first school Elisabeth attended was in Beckum. After finishing her exams, she left the Lyceum, which was three miles away in Ahlen, which she had attended from 1911 to 1913.

On March 8, 1930, Elisabeth Bahlmann and Otto Lagerfeld Jr. published a notice in the neighborhood Hamburger Nachrichten announcing their engagement. They were wed on April 11th, 1930 in Münster. Elisabeth was 32 years old and Otto was 48 at the time. The phrase "housewife" has been added next to the entry for Elisabeth Josef Emilie Bahlmann's sister Felicitas, who was one of the witnesses along with her husband Conrad Ramstedt. The marriage record on file in the Münster register office reads that Elisabeth Josef Emilie Bahlmann had "no profession," but it also claims that she had "no occupation." The modest wedding party is captured in a photograph standing in front of the structure on Dürerstraße. The bride and groom are beaming, the women are donning cloche hats, and the guys are donning top hats. The bride's mother is visibly proud that her younger daughter "married well," as they used to say back then: Her first son-in-law was a professor and her second son-in-law was a company director. The bride is surrounded by her siblings and their spouses.

The union had a good beginning. The economic crisis that allowed the Nazis to take a stronghold in the nation had little effect in Glücksklee. As a result, Otto Lagerfeld and Elisabeth were able to relocate further from the city center, where life was even more picturesque and serene. He bought the mansion at 4 Baurs Park on March 25, 1930, from Auguste Baur, the daughter of Georg Friedrich Baur, who had designed this lushly planted park bordered by grand homes. Soon after, on April 7, 1933, the family relocated to 3 Baurs Park, where they were treated to even more breathtaking views of the Elbe. Thanks to the steep slope that leads to the river, the view was unobstructed from beginning to end. But they couldn't fully settle there either, so when their children, Martha Christiane ('Christel'; born 1931) and Karl (born 1933), were still little, they moved from Hamburg to Bad Bramstedt.

Although it might appear that little Karl Otto grew up in a quiet neighborhood, that wasn't the truth. When his father was present, which admittedly wasn't often, he was preoccupied with his home expansion and renovation projects. His mother ran the home and gave the nanny and housekeeper instructions. In the barn next door, there were pigs and chickens, and there were cows grazing in the fields with their calves. Christel, Karl's older sister, enjoyed playing with the local boys, but most of the time Karl stood on the sidelines and daydreamed or drew in his sketchbook.

A gentle woman without children of her own, Karl's nanny Martha Bünz (b. c. 1907) showered the youngster with love. She and her husband resided in Bissenmoor and earned some extra cash by working for the Lagerfelds. According to Elfriede von Jouanne, her niece twice removed who corresponded with Karl Lagerfeld in the 1990s, "She got along with the boy, and he was fond of her." Karl's parents frequently had to be filled in by Martha Bünz. Elisabeth spent a good amount of time away, while Otto was perpetually busy. She accompanied her husband to the United States on a business trip from April 1 to April 29, for instance, and she did it again in 1950. Elisabeth Lagerfeld wrote to her mother in Münster in 1937 after returning from a protracted trip: "The children were delighted when I got back." Karl apparently repeatedly asked, "You're not going away again, are you?"

In addition to being born in July 1934, Karl Wagner grew up in Bissenmoor. He recalls the older sister of his acquaintance with affection: "Christel was a true tomboy. With us, she used to climb trees. We would remove the eggs from the crows' nests, blow them out, and thread the eggshells onto string. She seemed to be quite the contrast to Karl Otto, as he was known to his classmates and the neighborhood kids, who never participated in their activities. He would simply sit outside the house while we played in Bissenmoor, drawing and dressing his dolls. He reportedly grabbed the jointed puppets from a puppet theater that his half-sister, Thea, had received for Christmas one year and repeatedly dressed them in various outfits.

Karl Otto was obviously a very talented young man, especially in the language department. In 2015, he asserted, "I could speak German, French, and English at the age of six." "I had a private French tutor. Before World War I, she was a refugee who worked as a German teacher at a posh girls' school in France. I was eager to learn French because I was unable to understand either of my parents when they spoke the language. She taught me because she needed the cash. The neighbors must have been perplexed by this love for French since they would have seen it as an indication of unwarranted elitism and lofty educational aspirations. For instance, until far after World War II, the family of his childhood friend Siegfried Werner solely spoke Low German at home.

Karl reportedly started reading around age five. He began with the children's book Molle und der grüne Schirm before moving on to the German mythical epic Nibelungen. When he was older, he used to spend time in the attic flipping through copies of Simplicissimus, a pre-war German satirical weekly magazine. He enjoyed looking through his mother's mags as well. Paul Sahner recalls, "He would color in the black-and-white photographs with crayons because there were no picture books to buy at that time." He was able to hone his artistic abilities and sharpen his humor during these prolonged reading sessions in the attic. He was able to elicit a response and also give himself a safe haven by putting his thoughts on paper. He developed a detached air through his painting, one of someone who can fit anywhere but doesn't belong anywhere, who enjoys company but hovers above it all, and who participates in life but chooses to take his observations and feed them into his own symbolic world.

Karl wasn't at all down to earth like the neighborhood farmers' sons who had to help out in the fields and barn. Sylvia Jahrke remembers, "He was very intelligent and well-groomed." His fingernails were neat, I noted. The nails on the other boys' hands were black. She claims that he didn't have many friends and that the other kids didn't visit him at home. Sylvia said it appeared that the Lagerfelds were isolated from the outside world.

It's possible that Lagerfeld caught a peek of his future in Menzel's work. He might have seen a reflection of himself in the splendor of this king, whom Menzel avoided unduly glorifying and instead portrayed as a wise king in good company. According to art historian Werner Busch, "It is not only the composition that grants the king a central position; he also had a central role to play, namely that of arbiter." He granted his group of paid wits carte blanche, but he held onto the final say. Later, almost as if to pretend that the eighteenth century had never ended, Lagerfeld hosted round meals in both his château in Brittany and apartment on the Rue de l'Université. He constantly assessed his collections while seated at a huge table, surrounded by assistants, journalists, and dressmakers. This dapper ideal also anticipated his life as a creative director. Everyone had the right to express their views, but the wise king always had the final say.

Lagerfeld frequently discussed his aspirations as a child, portraying himself as a determined young man who would never accept anything less than the best. He described a persistent boy who used his imagination to transform a mundane existence in a rural area of northern Germany into a source of intrigue and escape. Little Karl imagined himself as Karl the Great, emulating his hero Frederick the Great.

There, the family stayed for a while. It was previously believed that the Lagerfelds only fled to Bissenmoor after the frequent air strikes on Hamburg started in late July 1943. Elisabeth Lagerfeld and the kids had actually been in the countryside for some time by this point. She informed her sister that she had purchased a rabbit hutch for her daughter in a letter she wrote from Bad Bramstedt to her sister in the summer of 1942. Additionally, eleven-year-old Christel informed her aunt in a letter that she and Mule were obtaining a small Christmas tree this year shortly before Christmas 1942. One was never present in Hamburg. In July 1943, Otto Lagerfeld joined them.

Since the British were on their way and change was in the air, the Lagerfelds would also experience the repercussions of the war. On July 18, 1945, Otto Lagerfeld sent a letter to the mayor of Bad Bramstedt informing him that on July 16, a British officer from the occupying forces (Captain Bruce of the "8 Corps District German Mobilization Center Control Unit") had ordered him to leave his home and the administrative building. There were 27 people impacted by this decision. Together with their families, he, the caretaker, and the foreman made a temporary abode in the cowshed of the Lagerfelds. Otto Lagerfeld asked for all three families to be given suitable housing in advance, knowing that the cows would need to be put back in the shed in late September. In addition, he requested the mayor build a storage building because the occupying forces had taken over the sheds used to store the grain and straw. "At the moment, the farm's open hearth is the only place I have to cook." On August 4, 1945, he received a response from the mayor stating that such housing was "no longer available."

The family had to begin residing in the cowshed as of July 15, 1945, before relocating to the granary. Finally, on February 15, 1946, after a grueling seven months, the mayor informed them that the structure had been "vacated by the British occupying forces" and they could immediately reclaim their residence. In a letter to the mayor dated March 9, 1946, Otto Lagerfeld methodically listed the costs of all the rental losses, damages, and other losses sustained, which came to a total of 3,084.37 marks in compensation. Evidently, he was compensated for the majority of the losses he had incurred. Then, on January 29, 1947, he made a list of the problems that the Bad Segeberg government had not yet resolved. The list listed "repairs for the radio apparatus and built-in gramophone" as well as "gymnastics equipment" that had been "removed and burned." For his trouble, he received 1,000 marks and 9,000 pounds of cocaine as "compensation in kind."

It would appear that hardships throughout the war and its aftermath affected even the Lagerfeld family. They were nevertheless fortunate compared to the millions that had a much worse fate. Fortunately, Otto Lagerfeld was too old and Karl Lagerfeld was too young to serve in the Wehrmacht. Although they undoubtedly went through times of terror and difficulty, they were never truly persecuted or displaced. They also avoided the majority of World War II's material costs. Hunger and poverty were widespread outside of the

Bissenmoor region, which was generally safe. Transport networks, houses, and businesses had all been damaged by the battle. The country's economy was in ruins. Little mouths were not satisfied by the school lunches served by the British military. The countless refugees from eastern Germany, who were frequently made to dwell in appalling conditions, were afflicted by the "winter of starvation" in 1946–1947, the coldest winter of the twentieth century in the North Sea region. Following the destruction of Germany's towns and cities, Ulrich Herbert notes that "the floods of refugees were directed first and foremost to rural regions." He notes that whereas the percentage of displaced individuals in Hamburg and Bremen was just 7% and 2% respectively, it was around 50% in the rural areas of Northern Germany.

Sylvia, a close friend of Karl's who left Bissenmoor in 1945 and moved back to the city with her family, had nutritional edema. Even though her father had survived the war, he was now barely able to provide for his family. At school, kids were talking about their horrible incidents. When they eventually returned, many of the men had been severely hurt or were still being kept as prisoners, and they were quite harsh with their boys, many of whom had been reared by women during their absence. Fortunately for Karl, this destiny was also avoided by the Lagerfeld family.

A personal portrait from 1938 shows that the Lagerfelds were one of many people who supported the Austrian Anschluss. It depicts the Bissenmoor residence and a nearby flagpole with a swastika flag floating at least twenty feet in the air. In the foreground, a young Karl Lagerfeld can be seen sporting a knit sweater, a pair of shorts, and knee-high socks. Standing on the lawn, the four-year-old is gazing at the home and the flag that is being waved by the wind.

In the instance of the Lagerfelds, the choice to fly the flag was not solely motivated by a sense of obligation. A message on the back of the image, which was processed at Photo Hoffmann in Bad Bramstedt, makes this statement. It appears to be written in Elisabeth Lagerfeld's handwriting and reads, "In memory of March 12, 1938." There is also a brief, partially visible description: "Chr. is standing by the flagpole checking the flag." Little Christel can be seen standing in the background next to the flagpole in the picture with her head pointing upward. It suggests support for the government and its most important symbol that a photo was taken to commemorate the annexation and that the day itself was thought to be a memorable occasion.

After the war was finished, he made an effort to establish himself as a regime critic. He stated to the denazification committee on July 24, 1947, "As a representative of American interests, my relationships with the party were extremely tense," noting problems with the dairy commissioner, the primary organization for the German dairy industry, and the Dairy Federation. The German government built a complex network of regional marketing groups and national organizations for all agricultural products with the adoption of the new Hereditary Farm Law in 1933. With nearly unlimited authority, these groups were able to regulate everything from prices, volumes, and quality standards to production, packing, shipping, and distribution. Companies who process milk were compelled to work with the new method.71 Otto Lagerfeld must have been concerned about letting Glücksklee slip from his grasp.

School was not something Karl Otto Lagerfeld enjoyed. He wasn't a particularly good student, found most topics boring, sang off-key in music class, struggled in physical education, and was frequently the target of jokes from his peers. And to make matters worse, it took over 1.5 miles to walk from Bissenmoor to the Jürgen-Fuhlendorf school.

Karl also thought that going to school was unnecessary. He once said, "I was hardly ever at school." "I didn't have to leave. It wasn't too tough to keep up with the others in rural Bad Bramstedt because there wasn't much competition there. But his former classmates have various recollections of events. For example, Ursula Scheube recalls her former classmate as a "completely normal pupil, not super gifted."

In a strict sense, he was fortunate to have the opportunity to go to school in the first place. According to Christel Friedrichs, who was given the name Christel after Karl's sister, "you had to have the right parents if you wanted to go to secondary school." Siegfried Werner, her father and Karl's next-door neighbor, "was the son of a farmer, which meant that was never a possibility for him." Things were different for the Lagerfelds since they never had a problem with money. However, it was probably too much to ask for any ten or twelve year old child to consider coming to school as a lucky break.

Later, as Karl grew close to his classmate Dorothee Großekettler (née Böge; 1934–2012), the trip to school got simpler. From Bissenmoor, one could easily walk to Kurhaus station, which was located along the AKN train route connecting Altona, Kaltenkirchen, and Neumünster. The two kids then proceeded to the following stop, Bad Bramstedt station. Their "private secondary school," established on May 1st, 1908, was nearby and convenient due to its location near the train station. Additionally, having his buddy Dorothee along for the ride was sure to make the distance seem shorter. Karl bravely followed her while the other people made fun of the "bride and groom" jokes. For Dorothee, the only girl he claimed to have been truly interested in at the time, he once sketched a Punch and Judy for her. Dorothee was a nice, social child from a good household, according to her former classmates. It's logical to suppose that Karl Otto's parents would have been aware of the fact that her father served as the clinic's director.

In 1937, the secondary school adopted the Jürgen-Fuhlendorf-Schule moniker. The Fleckenvorsteher (mayor) Jürgen Fuhlendorf, a local hero who "saved the farmers of Bad Bramstedt from serfdom in the seventeenth century," served as the model for the new name, which was ultimately considered appropriate for the institution. When World War II started, more and more students began to arrive at the institution. To avoid the frequent air attacks over Hamburg and Neumünster, families were moving to quiet neighborhoods or at the very least enrolling their kids in local schools there. The Jürgen-Fuhlendorf-Schule had 72 students in 1939; by 1944, there were 253.

Heinz-Helmut Schulz, who was his art instructor, was also pleased by his abilities. According to Barbara Dieudonné, "He completely accepted Karl Otto and encouraged him." According to Schulz, Karl caught his attention "because even at a young age, he had an ability to work independently." But even Karl's encouraging teacher had to deal with his student's cutting remarks. Karl was skilled at drawing people, but Schulz, who liked painting landscapes, told him: "You'll never be a landscape artist." He received the following reply from his pupil: "I wouldn't want to be [any good] if that meant drawing the kinds of pictures you do." Karl steered clear of landscapes entirely. Karl Lagerfeld would remember Schulz for the rest of his life since this significant individual was one of the few from Bad Bramstedt he kept in touch with after relocating to France.

Karl Otto has his own universe. He didn't make trouble with youthful mischief, harass the teachers, or smoke by the small shed outside the school like the other boys did. "As well as looking upper-class, he behaved that way, perhaps unintentionally drawing attention to the fact that he was different because he came from the city," says former classmate Peter Bendixen. "He seemed like some kind of messenger from a foreign land." His mannerisms revealed his privilege: "He was polite, well-behaved, and always extremely well-dressed," recalls Barbara Dieudonné. According to Inge Ludwig, "He was the only boy at the school ball to ask other mothers to dance." And he cherished his time with the girls.

With the guys, he acted in a different manner. His ability to be sarcastic is demonstrated by one incident from his former classmate Fritz Andresen. After the war, many kids wore out-of-date clothing since their families couldn't afford to buy new ones and money was tight. The situation was as it was because everyone was content with their meal. According to Inge Ludwig, "We refugees were given clothes that had been stitched together from hand-me-downs." Many people were wearing army jackets, and shoes were scarce.

When the school building was temporarily used to shelter refugees in April 1945, the final pandemonium of the war, instruction came to an abrupt halt. On November 28, the military administration ordered that classes begin, with "woeful resources," in the words of Peter Bendixen, a former classmate of Lagerfeld. The teachers at the school were forced to forfeit 25% of their pay from January 1, 1949, to March 31, 1950, as a result of the protracted nature of the situation. The private school eventually relocated to a nicely sized new building on the hillside in 1972 after transitioning to a state-funded selective secondary school in the 1950s. The previous building was converted into the Grundschule am Bahnhof, a primary school. The scientific labs continue to act as a reminder of the building's former use as an elite secondary school decades later.

The others weren't like Karl Otto. Both he and his classmates could feel it; they just didn't know what to call it yet. Two school pictures from 1948 show the difference clearly. One of these depicts him smiling while seated in the front row, one knee crossed over the other, and surrounded by the other lads in his class. In his dark double-breasted jacket with a peak lapel, he sticks out from the crowd. When you look at the photo closely, you can see that the youngster is wearing a signet ring on his right hand, which is an unusual ornament for a boy of his age and an indication of his lineage. The other image was captured during a school outing to Laboe in Kiel, a tourist town on the Baltic Sea, in August. Karl has on slacks, a tie, and a double-breasted jacket whereas the other kids on the boat are all dressed in shorts. He is the lone person seated in the picture. He looks directly into the camera, as though he is conscious of his allure. He has well styled hair. The breeze from the Baltic Sea has raised the hair of the other boys.

the hairstyle. In the sunlight, the young Karl's expertly styled hair positively gleams. According to Karl Wagner, the traditional Hitler Youth hairdo that so many guys had at the time was "buzzed sides and long hair on top." "Whereas his hair was pomaded and swept back." The majority of youngsters in northern Germany had blond or mousy hair, but one young kid stood out from the throng with his dark mane. Other boys began to grow their hair out after the war, but there was still one significant difference.

Being gay was of no great significance in his parents' eyes. When he was eleven years old, he inquired about homosexuality with his mother. She said, "Some people are this way, some are that way." "Some people have dark hair, some people have blonde hair," and so forth. Likewise, "It's like having a certain hair color, nothing more. What does it matter to people who are civilized? In his own words, he didn't have any trouble accepting the fact that he was gay. "I was fortunate to have very accepting parents. And I don't think they were all that naive when they were kids, either. He was essentially allowed to do what he liked. Although it might have been illegal for some people, nothing was prohibited where I lived.

In 2009, the Wirthweins discovered something, and they wrote to Karl Lagerfeld in Paris to inform him about it. They didn't hear from him again; well, this fashion designer wasn't one for looking back on the past. Since then, the pair has received four-figure offers for the book, but they are unlikely to sell it. In any event, the book illustrates several lines of familial and religious heritage. When it comes to the "resurrection of Prussia" that Karl Otto's godfather referred to in his dedication, Karl Lagerfeld, the Prussian monarch, brought it back to life in the person he became: "Basically it's true: I'm Prussian by nature."

Maybe the footage from the Hotel Esplanade didn't even include the youthful Karl Lagerfeld. Three shows were held over the course of two days, according to the invites in the Dior archives 168: two at evening galas on December 12 and 13, 1949, and one at an afternoon tea event at 4:00 on December 13. At the time, Lagerfeld had just graduated from high school, and he frequently recalled going to one of these performances with his mother. He had a sort of insight after the event. He wasn't entirely sure what to do with his artistic abilities before that. But when he attended the show and saw the creations of one of the greatest fashion designers in history, his eyes were opened to possibilities he had never thought were even possible.

At this Dior presentation, the outfits on exhibit were genuine works of art. The taffeta, silk, brocade, and velvet gowns, the furs, the sequin necklaces, the beading, and the gemstone embroideries, as well as the models' composure, deft twirls, and exaggerated postures, enthralled the crowd. The fact that he only uses a few basic colors—black, red, brown, and their pastel tones—and that he combines them in a way that is so drenched in unexpected beauty and sensational sophistication that they are met with cries of excitement and admiration in the banquet hall, according to a piece in Die Zeit, is significant. As instructed by the boss, the emcees merely muttered the names of the costumes into the microphone—"Poudre et Sucre," "Matisse," and "Christian Bérard"—without making any additional remarks. There are certain spots in the footage where it appears to be fogged up from cigar smoke entering the camera.

According to Der Spiegel, Dior's designs impressed the audience more for the "simplicity of the lines" than for their "extravagance." Constanze's assessment was that "the dresses were devoured by the women with their eyes," but that "not only the dresses" attracted the attention of the men in the crowd. The "ravishing girls from Paris," who "captured the flair of that enchanting city with their spectacular gowns, racy fragrances, and sparkling jewelry," were lauded by Die Zeit as "emissaries of a world that is still out there, somewhere: the big, wide world where there is no wreckage, no work—only parties, air travel, and formal dances."

This statement resembled a prophecy in certain ways. Karl Lagerfeld attended the presentation and was impressed by what he saw. In the future, he would undoubtedly elevate French and German ready-to-wear fashion to a whole new level. He told German Vogue, "I can still clearly remember the Dior show," before traveling to Hamburg to commemorate Chanel's Métiers d'Art show at the Elbphilharmonie in December 2017. This significant production was a late answer to the ancient master, coming over seven decades later and also right before Christmas. The Chanel presentation was superior to the storied Dior show. The big idol of his youth had long since been outrun by this Hamburg lad.

Lagerfeld's passion was fashion. After seeing the Dior show, he had one more experience that dispelled any remaining uncertainties. His mother approached the director of the Hamburg Academy of Fine Arts in Lerchenfeld and showed him some of her son's sketches as encouragement for his creative abilities. The director informed her that her son was not at all interested in art; rather, he was interested in fashion rather than inviting him to try out for the academy. Look closely at the striking costumes he depicts. He might work as a theater costume designer. Later, the child was forced to admit that "my sketches were not up to the standards of painting at that time."

His mother scolded him, "You're too lazy, you have no ambition, and you don't try hard enough to make something of yourself."

Karl's situation wasn't looking bright in the beginning of the 1950s. His lack of artistic desire had let down his mother, and nothing he achieved could make his father happy. He might have even felt disappointed in himself for not being able to make his aspirations come true. Though nothing was easy, he did have a general idea of what he wanted to do—after all, Dior had shown him what was possible. During his early years, he had gone through an odd incubation period. He merely had to wait for the idea to mature now that it had taken root. There was only one solution: He had to go to a new planet to realize his ideals.

These kinds of expectations were not exclusive to Karl Lagerfeld at this time. Many other young Germans desired to improve the negative perception of their country. Some people were lured to the realm of fashion, such as former anti-aircraft auxiliary F. C. Gundlach (born 1926), who used fashion photography to take his countrymen to exquisite visual worlds they had never even imagined. Wolfgang Joop (born in 1944), whose father insisted on discipline and obedience and who returned from the war late, rebelled against this rigid upbringing and found refuge in the made-up worlds of art and fashion. The age of the supermodel is credited to the photographer Peter Lindbergh, who was born in Reichsgau Wartheland (German-occupied Poland) in 1944 and raised in Duisburg as the offspring of exiled parents. And Jil Sander, who was born in 1943 and lived through the difficulties of post-war living about forty kilometers from Bad Bramstedt, would develop her impeccable style through the years.

For the young Karl Lagerfeld, fashion also held up the possibility of a life of greater significance. It provided an alternative reality to the mundane realities of daily existence—a more liberated, open way of life than his father's limited perspective. And fashion avoided wallowing in the tangles of German guilt, instead looking ahead with each new season.

Chapter 2:
Start a career (1952 to 1982)

Paris is up next. Karl Lagerfeld allegedly rode a train from Hamburg to the Gare du Nord on August 28, 1952. "I came here to complete two years of secondary education. However, I really stayed in Paris for a little bit longer than that. In a different version of the event, he flew there and was met by his father's business partners at the airport. In fact, the head of Carnation's French office, a colleague of his father's from work, took care of him no matter the mode of transportation. The young man was placed in lodgings at the Hôtel Gerson, which was situated across from the Sorbonne library at 14 Rue de la Sorbonne, by "a horrible woman with googly eyes," the secretary of the evaporated milk company's Paris office. While Lagerfeld would have been nineteen years old on September 10, 1952, he later claimed that this was a house "for minors and students" to give the idea that he had gone to Paris at the age of fourteen.

He didn't seem anxious or terrified at all in this strange city. In an interview that was captured near the end of his life, he discussed this: "People remarked to my mother, 'You know, it's harmful. He'll get lost, However, according to my mum, only a small percentage of individuals actually get lost. My son is from the group of people who don't get lost. "I mean, back then, nothing was dangerous, so you weren't afraid of anything," he said. Today is not like that. In addition, he was perched on the fifth story in one of his two apartments with a balcony, floating above everything; his existence was like the French movie Under the Paris Sky. He encountered a bustling student neighborhood full of stores and cafés when he left his rooms and stepped down onto the street below.

He constantly changed addresses even when he was a young man. He relocated to 32 Rue de Varenne in 1955. Then, in 1957, he relocated to 31 Rue de Tournon, where author Katherine Mansfield formerly resided, possibly to avoid the watchful eye of his landlady: "Finally I had my own flat in a building from the 18th century! There was nobody around to "keep an eye on me." Finally, I was free to act as I pleased. At 19 Rue Jacob, he had a unit with a view of the courtyard where he resided in 1958 and 1959. He once remarked, "The view of the gardens and Delacroix's studio was very poetic." Then, from 1959 to 1963, he lived in the same building as Voltaire, on the ground level of 7 Quai Voltaire: "You could never open the windows in summer because there was so much noise from the traffic."

At the Alliance Française, a cultural center that offers French classes to visitors, Lagerfeld honed his language skills. The student apparently attracted the teacher's attention since he said, "The good woman suggested that I help her with the courses for German pupils, but I told her that wasn't why I had come to Paris." In the city, he preferred to be active: "I spent all my time walking about. I could give tours of Paris! I also went to the movies to practice my French accent, from the very first showing to the very last. He asserted that he watched the 1950 movie Les Enfants Terribles, which was adapted from the tragic novel by Jean Cocteau about an incestuous brother and sister, five times in one day.

Less than 300 feet separated him from his first flat and "Le Champo," a restaurant on the corner of Rue des Écoles. The arthouse movie theater was a school for the visual arts before it erected a second screening room in the basement in 1956. Some of the future stars of French cinema, notably Claude Chabrol and François Truffaut, both of whom were a little older than Lagerfeld, frequented this small theater with its striking art nouveau façade. The young man also went to the French Film Institute and the theaters on the Champs-Élysées. He particularly likes older movies that transported him back to the 1930s. "I visited the theater as often as I could. I saw The Cabinet of Dr. Caligari and every other movie starring Gloria Swanson. After that, I had trouble sleeping for three nights because I was afraid that the puppet would kill me by entering my room from the balcony.

It appears that the young Karl explored the city's streets and arcades aimlessly to get to know it. The young German in Paris fit the definition of the flâneur given by Walter Benjamin in his Passagen-Werk (Arcades Project): "Dialectic of flânerie: on the one side, the man who feels himself viewed by all and sundry as a true suspect and, on the other side, the man who is utterly undiscoverable, the hidden man." Lagerfeld was able to give in to his want to people-watch anonymously since he was readily stimulated visually and even called himself a "voyeur"—even if he was also surreptitiously being watched by others. He thought the city looked like it belonged in a 1930s silent movie like Under the Roofs of Paris. Because of all the coal heating at the time, Paris was a dismal, almost scary city. The world's most beautiful city didn't seem especially clean on the stroll from the train station to the city center. He later remarked that the biggest changes since then had been in the colors and fragrances.

In a city where private life takes place on the streets, these early years in Paris were a time of travel and apprenticeship. The street becomes an interior for Parisians, according to Walter Benjamin.18 The young Karl could frequently be seen leisurely strolling around the city, not like a worker rushing for the metro or a tourist trying to locate the appropriate street, for he had no school to attend and no employment to speak of. Later, he described how different social strata would coexist in a neighborhood or even an apartment building, adding to the excitement of life. He walked from street to street in this public place, finding his way. As he crossed the Seine bridges to the Right Bank, he would stroll through the Louvre, through the Tuileries Garden, and the arcades of Rue de Rivoli. He would loiter by the windows of the book stores and antique stores of Saint-Germain-des-Prés. During his travels, he traveled across entire eras, retracing the steps of the existentialists who had gathered in the Café de Flore and admiring the splendor of the Louvre, which had been the royal residence until Louis XIV transferred his court to Versailles in 1682.

These lengthy strolls he took as a young man also influenced his later work. Just fifteen years prior, in his philosophical shards, Walter Benjamin stated that "the flâneur is the observer of the marketplace." His expertise is comparable to the occult study of industrial oscillations. He is a spy for the capitalists working in the consumer sector. And in fact, during his career as a designer, this people-watcher would frequently refer to his memory to find methods to profit from the zeitgeist. His motivation completely changed as he walked through the streets of his imagination and thought of the places he had been.

He gradually but steadily got his bearings in Paris. Peter Bermbach, a German student who had lived in the city from the mid-1950s and opted to move there in 1960, was one of the acquaintances he made along the road. They connected right away. He hadn't completed his Abitur, possibly because he was so confident in himself, but Bermbach remarked that he was quite knowledgeable. He enjoyed reading and listening to music. Karl quizzed the expertise of his new acquaintance: "Have you heard of Elisabeth Charlotte, Princess Palatine?" Yes, Bermbach had seen the obscene letters written by the princess who had wed Louis XIV's homosexual brother. The following day, we became buddies.

Additionally, there were some unspoken similarities between the two young men. A week had passed since Peter Bermbach had been imprisoned in Munich on suspicion of "attempted seduction" in accordance with section 175a of the German Criminal Code. The "gay paragraph" was vigorously enforced in the fledgling republic of West Germany, outlawing all homosexual conduct between men. The definition of a punishable offense then amended with the 1969 revision to include having sexual relations with a male who is under the age of twenty-one. The paragraph wasn't entirely eliminated until 1994, which was a recent year. However, life was already easier for gay men in more liberal France, where the age of consent had been twenty-one since August 6, 1942. Gay issues were never discussed, according to Bermbach. He left for the land of freedom, equality, and fraternity because of the ongoing legal danger because homosexuality was more accepted there.

When he started this new phase of his life, Karl Lagerfeld must have gone through a similar sensation. Didier Eribon, a sociologist, claims that he was approaching the stage where all of the childhood wounds "nourish the energies through which gay people create or re-create personalities for themselves."Finally, Lagerfeld had arrived in a culture where being gay was accepted. In 1996, he claimed that "the benefits of the fashion world are the absence of racism and homophobia."

France had to put up with the occupying forces' tyrannical presence and the Germans' degrading treatment. The horror reign of Germany grew worse the more fiercely France resisted the occupiers. Before the Allied Forces and the resistance fighters successfully liberated France from the grip of the Germans, more than 20,000 members of the resistance movement were slain in the liberation battles. The era that President Charles de Gaulle referred to as the "Thirty Years' War"—which spanned from the outbreak of World War I in 1914 to the "Libération" in 1944—finally came to an end in September 1944. Peter Bermbach frequently detected some reluctance on the part of the French. We two Germans got along well since we were also social outsiders.

In Karl's apartment at 7 Quai Voltaire, the two pals spent a lot of time together. According to Bermbach, "He lived in a furnished ground-floor flat with high ceilings." The bedroom was only five feet tall and reached by a narrow stairway without a banister. "Black and white stuff lined the space. As we listened to music, we would lay there on the bed as if we were two pals from high school. 33-rpm records were laying around the area in heaps. This area of the apartment was known as "the Oblomov room," after the character in Ivan Goncharov's calm and well-bred novel from the nineteenth century.

Karl was constantly advancing his musical knowledge. "Once, when I was in Madrid, I bought a record called Concertos for Two Organs by the baroque musician Antonio Soler, also known as Padre Soler," says Bermbach. Karl was eager to acquire it despite having never heard of it before. The record wasn't for sale in Paris, and we lacked the tools to produce a clone. He then proposed that we exchange albums: I would give him my Padre Soler and he would give me his new record of Lotte Lenya songs. Today, I still possess the Lenya record.

Even his maiden foray into the realm of high fashion seemed smooth thanks to Karl Lagerfeld. The International Wool Secretariat (IWS), a marketing group predominantly representing Australian wool producers, was well-known to both lovers and students of fashion in

Paris. The IWS organized a competition for young designers as part of its activity in Paris, promoting virgin wool at a time when synthetic fibers were becoming more popular. Sketches from aspiring designers were requested in the hopes of being hired as a designer's assistant. On giant posters with a fashion illustration by René Gruau in 1954, the phrase "Concours du Dessin de Mode" was prominently displayed.

Karl's luck must have been better than that of the other applicants. Later, the designer would assert that he made no preparations at all for the contest. "I had entirely forgotten that I had submitted a design for a coat by the time I got a telegram six months later telling me I had won a prize. I despise coats. Even though they were tailored, he claimed to have given away many of his own coats. Otto Lagerfeld once insisted on buying his son a coat due to the cold weather when Karl went to meet him at the appropriately upscale Hotel George V where his father was staying when he was in Paris. Karl obviously didn't think twice about expressing his desires. He maintained that it had to be that coat or nothing at all, pointing out a navy blue cashmere coat in the shop across the street. Of course, he obtained his objectives. My father gave in to all of my requests.

As the Woolmark Prize deadline approached on October 31, aspiring designers anxiously sent in their fashion illustrations in the hopes of winning. The top designs from the three categories were then created at the ateliers of three fashion designers: Hubert de Givenchy created the gown, Pierre Balmain created the suit, and Jacques Fath created the coat. Not simply because the young man who detested jackets was named the winner of the category for coats, but also because it happened on December 11, 1954, would make the evening a memorable one.

At the cocktail function, the three victors were seated on the stage. In addition to a gray felt hat and gray gloves, twenty-one-year-old Karl exhibited his canary-yellow coat, which had three-quarter-length sleeves, a deep V-shaped neckline at the back, and an eccentric belt-buckle collar. Later sneering, he said, "Very ladylike." "At the time, it appeared new." Another newcomer joined him up there on the stage: Yves Saint Laurent, who had finished third the previous year and was now receiving the award for best dress at the age of eighteen. They appeared like two well-behaved schoolboys in suits as Lagerfeld and Saint Laurent stood there with Colette Bracchi, the winner in the suits category, and the three models. They were thin and serious-looking. Karl the Great still had a youthful appearance. When he later claimed to be sixteen years old when he won the reward, he almost passed for that age. However, he was already sporting his distinctive adult appearance, which included a signet ring on his right ring finger and a white handkerchief in his breast pocket.

When Karl went to the Balmain workshop where the coat was being created for the award ceremony, Pierre Balmain gave him an opportunity to work as his assistant. Later, Lagerfeld admitted that Cristóbal Balenciaga (1895-1972) had also offered him a job, but he declined—possibly because he was turned off by the designer's rigid forms, persistent elegance, and monastic, clandestine ways—since he didn't want to begin his career there. Instead, Karl chose the younger designer Balmain (1914–1982), who achieved fame abroad in 1954 for creating the stunning gown with a flared skirt and a wasp waist that Audrey Hepburn wore to wed Mel Ferrer.

Before beginning his first employment with Balmain, young Karl had been living a somewhat aimless existence. The time has come to sharpen our concentration. He had no professional training in the field of fashion and was thus in for a shock: "I had my own idea about it all, but it was completely removed from reality," he later recalled. The young designer gained a foundational understanding of design principles at Balmain by studying "techniques from the 1920s and 1930s that no longer exist, for fifteen to twenty hours a day." He developed the skills necessary to create sketches that include all the information needed to make the garment while he was working at the fashion firm. No one will need to know the measurements, the spacing, the type of buttons to use, or where to place the sleeves because I can draw every last detail. Everything in the sketch is accurate and in the right place.

Karl Lagerfeld spent a lot of time in Paris working, but he also found time to meet new people. He first met Bronwen Pugh, one of his boss's muses, while he was working in the Balmain atelier. She was ranked alongside Marlene Dietrich, Vivien Leigh, and Greta Garbo by Pierre Balmain as one of the most beautiful women in the world. Pugh, who was born in London in 1930, debuted alongside a group of British models that included Barbara Goalen and Fiona Campbell-Walter. These new models signaled the beginning of the British fashion era, when stars like Twiggy and Jean Shrimpton embodied the ideal modern lady, and artists like Mary Quant and Ossie Clark caught the mood of the day. Even Parisian fashionistas might be seen looking for the newest fashions on Carnaby Street and later King's Road.

The youthful assistant at Balmain, Karl Lagerfeld, who is also a foreigner, got along well with Bronwen Pugh. She shared a home with models Svetlana Lloyd, a Russian-English model who worked as an in-house mannequin at Dior, and Christine Tidmarsh, an English model who was friends with Yves. In 1956, the three young ladies hosted supper for both aspiring fashion designers in their modest flat with a view of the Eiffel Tower. The designers showed up at the flat-share on Avenue de la Bourdonnais believing they were going to a formal sit-down supper, Pugh subsequently said. But (a) we didn't have any money, and (b) all we had was this tiny apartment without any seats. So instead, we placed a few cushions on the ground. They were courteous yet surprised when they showed up. A nice evening dinner is very popular in France.

Through Bronwen Pugh, Karl also got to know Victoire Doutreleau, one of Christian Dior's preferred mannequins. According to Doutreleau, "She introduced us at the Bar des Théâtres on Avenue Montaigne." She could see that Karl liked her right away because he said, "We were both still kids, you know. Although he had a romantic side, he was still a person with a strong personality. She enjoyed his French accent, and she was always astounded by how rapidly he switched topics. It wasn't long before he gave her the nickname "Vichnou." Victorie is depicted modeling garments from all different eras in Lagerfeld's 1956 drawing, "Victoire à toutes ses époques," as if she had journeyed through time from the "Lady of the Camellias" to Coco Chanel, from the Belle Époque to the present.

The big drawing is still prominently displayed on the wall of her Paris flat.

Dior was the shared factor, thus. Victoire Doutreleau, a model, and Anne-Marie Poupard (later Muoz), a coworker at the atelier whose uncle, musician Henri Sauguet, was a friend of Christian Dior, were introduced to each other by Yves Saint Laurent's assistant, Dior. According to Doutreleau, who had a strong sensual allure, "I was already one of the star mannequins when Yves came to Dior in 1955." They were a close-knit bunch; Yves stayed in touch with Victoire for a long time and Anne-Marie for a long time. He brought Anne-Marie with him when he established his own fashion business on Rue Spontini, and she remained his most crucial worker up until his 2002 retirement from the industry. The moment was great, adds Doutreleau. There was no animosity between Karl and Yves back then. However, in the long run, a design god like Yves Saint Laurent would be unwilling to accept the presence of another god. It worked both ways.

He enjoyed his new pals. Like him, they were successful, youthful, and attractive. At last, he was rubbing shoulders with influential people, mingling with sophisticates and former Dior models—the kind of women who held their cigarettes at a perfect angle between their delicate fingers. The experience was fantastic. These talented young people were in high demand, and the fashion industry was flourishing. Dior was the talk of the world, while certain people were obsessive over Balmain. Karl was delighted and proud to have gone so far in such a short period of time from the north German lowlands.

Additionally, Karl had found a similar soul in fellow designer Yves Saint Laurent. He also originated from a totally distinct world. On August 1, 1936, he was born in Oran, a coastal city in Algeria, where his father Charles Saint Laurent controlled an insurance firm and a chain of movie theaters. The family was comfortably affluent because the grandparents of both Charles and his wife Lucienne Andrée had fled Alsace for North Africa during the Franco-German War of 1870–1871. His mother sported fitted attire and read French fashion magazines. Like Karl when he was younger, Yves kept to himself, drew, was tormented at school, and dreamed of living in

Paris. The French Algerians, known as colons (settlers), were frequently referred to as pieds noirs (black feet) beginning in the 1950s despite the fact that Yves was French.

But Yves and Karl, who believed they were destined for better things, what did fate have in store for them? Together, they visited a clairvoyant on a mezzanine in the Rue de Maubeuge in order to learn their destination. Lagerfeld remembered, "She was a fat Turkish woman with the most beautiful turquoise eyes." Although she noted that it would "end quite quickly," she foresaw enormous success for Yves, while Karl's actual success wouldn't come until it was all over for the rest.

Karl regarded such forecasts as absolute truth. His mother and aunt had visited the fortune-tellers at the Send, a fair that travels to Münster three times a year, and they had told him that they took clairvoyance very seriously. In the state of Münster, fortune-telling was a widespread occurrence that even found its way into literature in the shape of a poem written by German poet, novelist, and musician Annette von Droste-Hülshoff in the nineteenth century. Karl frequently traveled with his mother to Münster to see his aunt Felicitas and cousin Tita. He would share their belief in the existence of second sight. He took the Parisian fate teller seriously after hearing what she had told him. He said, "The things she foretold happened. After that, I visited her every two years, and I never made a significant choice without her. The phone rang in my automobile one day in 1987. "I see that you're on your way to sign a contract," remarked Madame. There is a mistake on page 7 that will work against you. She was accurate. An error had been made by a secretary.

On October 24, 1957, everything changed in an instant when Christian Dior passed away in Montecatini, Italy, from a heart attack. Nobody anticipated that, and he was just 52 years old. But operations had to continue, therefore Yves Saint Laurent, the designer's teenage assistant, was named as his replacement right away. At the late designer's funeral in Paris, which was essentially a national event with thousands of mourners in attendance, Yves and Karl grasped the importance of this job. At the funeral at Callian in the South of France, Yves had a solemn expression on his face. Without further ado, the youthful couturier made his debut for France's most prestigious fashion brand on January 30, 1958, at the age of just 21. The quiet young man won praise for his daring "trapeze line," a more fluid design with narrow shoulders and a wide hem that marked a departure from his forebear's distinctive nipped waist.

None of these individuals had any idea that Yves Saint Laurent would be drafted into the military on September 1, 1960, or that he would soon be admitted to the military hospital due to "nervous depression." They had no clue that the care he would get in the mental health unit would make him a nervous wreck—or that he would abruptly lose his position at Dior and be replaced by Marc Bohan. Victoire Doutreleau recalls, "It was so awful." It's like putting a swan in a cage with meowing cats, Yves in the military, I said.

But all of that was yet to come. It was 1958, and Yves was having a fantastic time. From assistant to creative director, from loner to lover, from relative unknown to the bright star of Parisian society, he had advanced rapidly in just one year. Karl missed the mark. Even though he was still only an assistant, an unknown, and a loner, time was on his side, as his fortune-teller had said.

Karl Lagerfeld left Pierre Balmain in 1958 because he was getting bored with his job there and moved to Jean Patou on Rue Saint-Florentin. He claimed that despite everyone's advice to the contrary, he was more interested in taking leadership there than in continuing as an assistant at Balmain. The most significant development was that, like Yves at Dior, he would now serve as the artistic director of a fashion house. However, Jean Patou's brand was neither as well-known or as significant as Dior. Jean Patou, who passed away in 1936, is most remembered for incorporating sportswear into haute couture and for his iconic Amour Amour and Joy scents from the 1920s and 1930s, respectively. It was more so a little somber. Raymond Barbas, Patou's brother-in-law, who admired the young man they called "Monsieur Charles" in the studio, directed the commercial. The designer first opted to use the more exotic-sounding name Roland Karl to make his haute couture lines.

The cover of the German weekly publication Münchner Illustrierte featured an even more dashing-appearing Karl. As he stands close to the model Kara in the photo, the "new man at Jean Patou" is seen gesturing. As a mark of his occupation, he wears a pincushion on his left wrist.55 Even while he may have appeared happy in the shot, the designer soon understood that Patou wasn't where he had discovered true contentment. "But I reminded myself that you are not here to be an art critic; rather, you are here to learn. Get rid of it and move on. My plan was to simply put in more hours than the others and render them unnecessary. And it succeeded.56 But he was running out of patience. In a later stage of his career, he remarked, "I felt like I was in an old people's home."57 Only two couture collections per year, each with sixty or seventy garments, were required of him. For this aspirational young designer, this simply wasn't enough. He wanted to stretch his wings since he was growing more and more interested in ready-to-wear garments. "Ultimately, that's why I became a freelance designer, which was unusual in the early 1960s," he remarked. He was pleased to declare that following his time at Patou, he "was never employed again—by anyone!"

His father gave him a rather basic Volkswagen convertible for Christmas when he got his first automobile. Although it was green, he had a dark blue paint job done on it since he didn't want to drive around Paris in a green automobile that had a German license plate. He was then given a Mercedes 190 SL convertible by his parents. It was the only vehicle of its kind in the entire city of Paris, and I was operating it. Everyone in the community knew who I was because of the convertible, which made me famous. Today, I would be really embarrassed by that kind of behavior. The automobile had red leather seats and was cream in color. Because Rosemarie Nitribitt, a high-end escort who was brutally killed in Frankfurt in 1957, had also driven one, the model was known as the "Nitribitt Mercedes" in Germany. The fact that this name was brought up frequently created a misconception in Germany that Lagerfeld actually drove the same automobile, even though it was merely the same model. A separate tale is the fate of the "Nitribitt Mercedes" itself.

When Karl went out with the top down, he frequently left his 190 SL parked outside of Deux Magots for hours at a time, according to Peter Bermbach. And if it wasn't there, he would be going about the neighborhood, stopping at the Boulevard Saint-Germain, the Café de Flore, and the Deux Magots before returning to the Boulevard, Saint-Benoît Street, and Rue de l'Abbaye. One-way streets weren't common back then, and buses and taxis didn't have their own lanes, according to Bermbach. Despite everything, driving around Paris was enjoyable. Karl was kind, upbeat, and supportive. Charles Simoni, who worked at the Lanvin fashion house and knew Karl, and another acquaintance from the fashion world were with Bermbach when he rented a car and drove out to the countryside. Their car broke down on Sunday in the early 1960s about 20 miles southwest of Paris, close to Trappes. When Bermbach couldn't find a garage, he called Karl from a bar and said, "Could you pick us up, please?" He arrived there an hour later in the large Bentley he was then known for.

More and more people started recognizing Lagerfeld in the neighborhood. He was often spotted picking up his stack of international newspapers and magazines from the kiosk on the corner of Rue Saint-Benoît, then heading to the Café de Flore to systematically leaf through the pages before getting back into his car to go for a spin. He liked to dine with friends at the Brasserie Lipp across the road. Soon they no longer had to sit with the tourists on the first floor. Miraculously, they always had a table downstairs— like French president François Mitterrand, who later became a regular at the establishment. Karl and his friends would occasionally head to the Montana Bar next to Flore with Françoise Dorléac, the older sister of Catherine Deneuve. "Karl loved her because she was loud and cheerful," Bermbach recalls. The actress, who made many films during her short career and worked with François Truffaut, Jean-Paul Belmondo, and Roman Polanski, died in a car accident on her way to the airport in Nice in 1967 at the age of twenty-five.

Karl and his pals benefited from this altered social dynamic. They discovered themselves in the center of the action. According to historian Matthias Waechter, "the Saint-Germain-des-Prés neighborhood in Paris served as one of the major intellectual hubs of the world from 1945 and was under the undisputed hegemony of Jean-Paul Sartre and Simone de Beauvoir, who epitomized the ideal of the modern intellectual." The fact that Yves and Karl frequently found themselves here at the same time as the existentialists was a really fortunate coincidence. These young fashionistas would not only be able to credit the new wave of consumerism for their futures, but also the broader social shift milieu. And Simone de Beauvoir, who challenged and redefined what it meant to be a woman in her 1949 book The Second Sex, may have best captured this social transformation. The founder of gender studies distinguished between biological gender and cultural imprint, revealed the socially prescribed motherly and caring responsibilities, and emphasized how males had traditionally viewed women as the "other" and an "object."

Fashion designers adopted this social shift with speed. In the 1950s, Yves and Karl were both still engaged in the prestigious field of haute couture, creating custom clothing for affluent customers. But in the 1960s, the designers dominated ready-to-wear fashion by providing a luxurious substitute for haute couture. This alternative not only made clothing options available to many more women, but it also gave fashion businesses access to much wider markets. Fashion was evolving to be more adaptable in line with rising freedoms, and there was a resurgence of interest in innovative, intriguing concepts. As time went on, designers had women at their feet rather than kneeling in front of clients and models to give a service. New trends were about to emerge as a new era ushered in. In a short period of time, the miniskirt worn with a sheer blouse would come to represent female liberty, and the "Le Smoking" tuxedo for women would stand for female empowerment.

Karl was aware that he needed to adapt to the times. He also understood that having the correct connections would be beneficial to him. When he appeared in the 1961 Françoise Sagan film Goodbye Again alongside Ingrid Bergman and Yves Montand, he was friendly with Anthony Perkins, who played the actor. Additionally, he frequently dined with Yves Saint Laurent on his houseboat near Neuilly. "The two of them were friends for a long time, without there being any jealousy," claims Peter Bermbach.

Following Pierre Bergé's arrival, Lagerfeld developed a dislike for the character. When Karl offered Bermbach a green angora jumper he had gotten as a present from Yves in the 1970s, Bermbach became aware that a fight was about to break out. He didn't want anything around him to make him think of his old pal.

The way Lagerfeld behaved wasn't to everyone's taste. Sometimes this young man, who was soon to become a household name, could be utterly haughty. He once received an invitation to supper from Azzedine Alaa, for instance. The Tunisian tailor was working as Comtesse Nicole de Blégiers' housekeeper and staying in her chambre de bonne. He requested permission from the aristocracy to host the dinner at one of her properties while she was gone. Yes, she said, "as long as you don't go crazy." At this meal in 1960, there were no wild antics, yet the whole thing had a nasty aftertaste. Along with Christoph von Weyhe, who was Alaa's companion from 1959 until the fashion designer's passing in 2017, Anne-Marie Muoz was undoubtedly present at the meal. The designer with the recognizable James Dean coif was seated across from the German art student. Despite the fact that they could have known each other for years, they had never met before. Weyhe's father was friends with Otto Lagerfeld and held property in the East Holstein community of Eutin. He also provided Glücksklee with milk. When Christoph relocated from Holstein to Paris, his father had informed him, "Otto's son is in Paris too." "You two ought to get to know each other." Because Lagerfeld only ever mentioned his parents' new home in Baden-Baden and because he claimed to be of Swedish ancestry, the two men that evening never even learned that they were from the same region.

For a very long time to come, Lagerfeld would keep telling this tale. In a 1990 appearance on French television, he even asserted that his father was a Swede. He claimed that although his father was a baron, he wasn't known by the prefix "von Lagerfeld" because it wasn't used in Sweden. On multiple instances, he also asserted that his father had spelled his last name "Lagerfeldt." He hadn't just come up with these concepts; they had a long history behind them. Despite coming from a phrase for a field where products were stored, the surname Lagerfeld is not Swedish in origin. Furthermore, it does not translate to "large field," as journalist André Leon Talley asserted in 1995. Talley mistakenly believed that Lagerfeld's close friend's Swedish surname was the French equivalent of Grand-Champ in Brittany, where Lagerfeld had purchased a château in the 1970s. In fact, the Swedish word lager, which is used in compound nouns for words like "bay leaf" and "laurel wreath," meaning "bay" or "laurel" A Swedish Jew named Israel Israelson (1610–1648) was given the noble surname Lagerfäldt in 1646. Over time, the spelling evolved, and the coat of arms for Lagerfeld(t) showed a luxuriant laurel tree with twelve red berries. Tönnies Lagerfeld(t), Karl's great-great-great-grandfather, is believed to have relocated to St. Pauli from Sweden around 1767. By the eighteenth century, this branch of the family tree had deleted the t from the end of the surname.

However, why did young Karl aspire to be a Swede? He might have wanted to avoid being referred to as a "boche" by the French. In any case, he enjoyed using his creative mind to enhance his past. He claimed to have grown up in a castle to American acquaintances he gained in the early 1970s through the cartoonist Antonio Lopez.78 Even farther, he moved the "family castle" to the "Danish border," which is actually around 60 miles away from Bad Bramstedt. He hid his background by changing his birthdate and his family history. This confident young guy rewrote time and space, creating his own version of the past to suit his needs. He created himself from the ground up, just like in a creation myth from the post-metaphysical era.

Karl Lagerfeld shielded himself by assuming a false identity. As a "false self" (C. G. Jung) or the theatrical masks worn in ancient Greece ("persona") to portray a certain character and conceal the wearer's identity, this would be referred to as a persona in the field of depth psychology. He adopted this role to act out socially acceptable behavior in this anti-German environment. A person neglects their inner life when they get overly identified with the persona they project for their public image, claims Jung. This could account for two characteristics that best characterized this fashion designer: his cult following and his mood swings. With the aid of the mask he wore, he was able to become an iconic figure, shield his "true self," and maintain his distance from other people. While this was going on, his neglected inner world showed itself in subtly aggressive behaviors that might have caused his sporadic outbursts.

In Baden-Baden, Elisabeth Lagerfeld got along well with her young neighbor. Mrs. Lagerfeld presented Marga Ullrich two crocheted pot holders and six miniature fruit knives with iridescent mother-of-pearl handles for her wedding in 1965. These kinds of wedding presents, which unmistakably attach the bride to the position of homemaker, might not be popular nowadays. The elderly woman who resided at 16a Hahnhofstrasse was a devout feminist, but she was also a sensible person who valued a clean, well-maintained home. Marga Ullrich was overjoyed by the presents. The fruit knives have never been used, and she still has the white and blue potholders.

It turned out that the Lagerfelds made good neighbors. They frequently stopped over to visit Marga Ullrich's parents on Sundays at around 11:00 a.m. After they left, Ullrich recalls Mrs. Lagerfeld's Dior perfume, which smelled of lily of the valley, continuing to linger in the stairway. She was distinguished at the time by her purple stockings and black Persian lamb fur coat, according to Ullrich. Occasionally, Otto Lagerfeld, who always wore a suit and tied his tie "in a thick knot," would bring some of his son's sketches with him. Josef Weis, Ullrich's father, was an ambitious painter who also worked at a savings bank in Baden-Baden. Otto politely asked Weis what he thought of the sketches, and he said that while the manner was quite different from that of his landscape paintings, the draftsmanship was "self-assured." Otto Lagerfeld seemed to be both pleased with his son and unsure of how to see his art and career, according to Marga Ullrich.

Naturally, Karl and Elizabeth were less concerned about the accident than the man who had paid for the cars. Later on, Lagerfeld remarked, "My mother and I died laughing." "My father never pardoned us for laughing so hard at that. I mean, I was able to wreck three cars in a single motion. The three vehicles were pressed together tightly.

Despite the fact that Lagerfeld commuted in various elegant vehicles, he wasn't the best driver. He had passed his driving test "without issues" when he was seventeen years old, but his trouble was that he was often distracted: "I was always looking out of the window," he stated. Instead than focusing solely on the road in front of me, I wanted to soak it all in. It was just too dull for me. When I have to stare straight ahead, I doze off. In addition, I am exhausted by that constant hum and the mind-numbing noise made by the wheels. not only in the automobile. I doze off anywhere, including on planes and trains.

The interview was Rosemarie Le Gallais' first significant one in Paris. The young woman, who was born in Lüdenscheid in 1937 and had grown up in Plettenberg, North Rhine-Westphalia, had left the picturesque Sauerland region for Paris in 1960. She was carrying on the tradition of her mother, who had lived there when she was younger and had given her daughters the notion of the city. Rosemarie studied French at the Alliance Française when she first moved there, where Karl Lagerfeld, who is now the designer at Chloé, had also attended classes a few years before. She was joined in the city by her sister, whose son Stefan Lubrina would, by pure coincidence, go on to work closely with the fashion designer many years later when his career as a set designer brought him to Chanel's major productions.

When one of her favorite fashion houses needed an attaché de presse in 1967, Rosemarie learned about it. Since purchasing a dress from Boutique Laura on Avenue du Général Leclerc, she had been a fan of Chloé. Sam Rykiel, whose wife Sonia Rykiel was still mostly unknown at the time, ran the store outside of the city. In reality, the knitted maternity clothing that Sonia had been making since her first pregnancy was still on display without a separate label when Rosemarie purchased the Chloé dress from the shop in the early 1960s. When Sonia launched her own shop on Rue de Grenelle, her knitwear quickly gained international recognition. She and Lagerfeld had a distinctive appearance as well as a fresh creative outlook. After Lagerfeld, Sonia was Saint-Germain-des-Prés's second-most well-known fashion icon thanks to her distinctive red hair. She belonged to a new generation of designers in Paris who, unlike this German, were not content with working as couturiers for the system but instead desired to be creators and leave their own imprint on the industry.

While working under Gaby Aghion in his early years, Lagerfeld remembered, "We were various designers and she coordinated it all. Every designer, including myself, was freelancing for other businesses, frequently in other countries—this was a new method of working at the time. A completely new method of collaboration between fashion firms and their designers was developed by Gaby Aghion. According to Géraldine-Julie Sommier, who oversees the Chloé archives, "couture assistants still played a supportive role in the 1950s." She wished to allow upcoming designers to fully express their ideas. It was almost as if Lagerfeld was designed for this new style of working as a freelance designer. Outside of haute couture, he had no need for direct consumer interaction because "everything is anonymous in ready-to-wear clothing; you're working with women you don't know." He wanted to collaborate with other companies in Paris and Italy at the same time. To him, his supervisor acted as a mentor. They frequently drove back to her home in the fifth arrondissement after work in the evenings to continue discussing fabrics, designs, and trends there. She would drop Karl off at her house, and he would walk home from there by cutting through the Latin Quarter and returning to the Rue de l'Université. Later, Lagerfeld claimed that the apartment at number 35, which he moved into in 1963, was where he "spent the ten happiest, most carefree years" of his life.

He also felt at home at Chloé since its mentality was more relaxed than that of other fashion firms, where manners were everything. Because she loved the roundness of the letters, Gaby Aghion named her label after a friend, Chloé Huysmans. Before launching her own collection, the young fashionista traveled in bohemian circles on the Left Bank. On November 29, 1957, she held her first unofficial fashion presentation in the Café de Flore, revealing her upcoming spring/summer collection while enjoying a croissant and coffee breakfast. The focus of Aghion's design was timeless, wearable apparel. With his wit and unique approach to fashion, Lagerfeld was perfect for Aghion. This brand was not interested in creating pretentious clothing for attractive hangers-on, the kind of women who clung to wealthy men and sat idly at cocktail parties. It was all about creating clothing for emancipated women who worked outside the home and supported themselves. At Chloé, classic elegance gave way to contemporary style. This fashion was all about having a good time, with its lightweight silk materials, knee-length styles, and whimsical accents like ribbons or a goofy hat. It was unprecedented in Paris in the 1950s and the early 1960s.

When Lagerfeld joined the company in 1964, the company had a great external reputation, but internally, things were still somewhat understated. According to Rosemarie Le Gallais, "It was a family business with a four-room apartment as its base of operations." Karl didn't even have a personal studio. Rolls of cloth were piled up against the walls of Jacques Lenoir's office when he arrived to complete the fittings, so Jacques Lenoir had to make room for him.

Even though Lagerfeld was creating designs at a rapid pace, haute couture was still very much alive and well in the background. The beautifully hand-painted gowns that are still on display in the Chloé archives on Rue de la Baume, many of which were influenced by art nouveau in the late 1960s, demonstrate the designer's desire to create more than just production-line clothing. Lagerfeld loved eccentric ideas, as evidenced by the fun tennis-themed tie he chose to wear with his pricey Cifonelli suit in 1971. The "Interplanétaire" garment for autumn/winter 1970, with its planet embroideries evoking the work of surrealist fashion designer Elsa Schiaparelli, and of course the pop art gowns he created for spring/summer 1971, one of which included a big cat pattern, were other examples. Even wearing sneakers, his models walked the runway in October 1974.

Additionally, Lagerfeld employed a ground-breaking approach to communication by inviting photographers like Helmut Newton, Deborah Turbeville, and Guy Bourdin to organize fashion shoots in his Place Saint-Sulpice apartment. It was advantageous for the photographers because it eliminated the need to rent studio space because of the fantastic shooting environment afforded by the high ceilings and floor-to-ceiling windows. Occasionally, the photographer just so happened to capture the designer, like in the February 1975 American issue of Vogue. This individual was an expert at promoting himself. The models, photographers, and journalists didn't hold this against him because he was so affable and welcoming. Instead, they were only appreciative of the opportunity to be a part of his expanding universe.

The free-spiritedness of the early 1970s was embodied in Lagerfeld's designs. His fashion shows are a case in this; according to former Vogue editor Ariel de Ravenel, "They were incredibly fun and lively." "Today's models stroll down the catwalk appearing melancholy, as opposed to when they danced. It was avant-garde and thrilling.The various faces on the catwalk thrilled Corey Grant Tippin, a close friend of Lagerfeld's, who said: "Pat Cleveland, Amina Warsuma, and Carol LaBrie on the runway: It was so diverse for the time." It also didn't end there. The story of an intriguing last-minute addition to the lineup is told by Bill Cunningham, the photographer who would eventually establish street style. Antonio Lopez, a friend of Lagerfeld's, was traveling to the Chloé show with a group of friends when he spotted a woman standing on the side of the road. After he forced the taxi to stop, he picked up the passenger and inquired about her interest in being a model for Lagerfeld's show. The woman, who later revealed herself to be a prostitute, was in favor of the plan. She was costumed for the presentation by Lagerfeld, who adored pleasant surprises like these; her debut for Chloé was "a sensation."

The diversity movement was strongly supported by this fashion designer. André Leon Talley, a reporter for Women's Wear Daily at the time, was one of the journalists traveling with him to Los Angeles for a Chloé show. When they arrived at the Beverly Hills Hotel to check in, the party of about ten to twelve persons were greeted with the following statement: "I'm afraid we have an issue. He cannot remain here. Talley was the only Black man in the group, and he was referred to as "this man" by him. In answer, Lagerfeld said, "We'll all leave then." Eventually, a deal was reached: Lagerfeld's group decided to remain, and Talley was given a room in one of the bungalows.

Beginning in the early 1970s, Lagerfeld always left the stage after the performance to take a bow. He was now focusing on his own reputation as the brand's face. Additionally, Gaby Aghion offered him unlimited freedom, but she didn't want any other individuals to receive attention. The idea of "Chloé by Karl Lagerfeld" was never considered because the fashion house itself was intended to shine rather than the particular designer. But the time for polite restraint had passed as more publications began to mention that Karl Lagerfeld had created the collection. Chloé eventually gave in and acknowledged Lagerfeld as the designer. When Jane Fonda was photographed by Jeanloup Sieff and put on the cover of French Vogue in February 1970, she was sporting a silk outfit designed by "Karl Lagerfeld pour Chloé."

Both designers drew inspiration from artists, but some of Lagerfeld's art-inspired designs for Chloé have not held up well over time. For instance, Oskar Schlemmer and Aubrey Beardsley prints now look extremely dated, in contrast to Yves Saint Laurent's "Mondrian" garment from 1965, which was more understated and successful. Piet Mondrian's "neoplasticism"'s rigid color and design aesthetic worked because it contrasted with the fluid, geometrically shaped forms of couture. It was actually just a formless sack garment, yet despite that, it came to represent the affinity between art and fashion. Of course, it was created by Yves Saint Laurent. Karl Lagerfeld was always second best. "Yves Saint Laurent was more successful in the 1970s," claims Ariel de Ravenel. Everyone was eager to visit. Chloé had come in second. However, one characteristic that set Lagerfeld apart was his sense of humor. The midnight-blue Chloé gown worn by Pat Cleveland in the autumn/winter 1979 show is possibly the best illustration of this. The garment, which is currently part of the Palais Galliera collection, has an appliqué of a lightbulb made of pearls and rhinestones on it. It was motivated by Lagerfeld's love of classic German design and pays homage to Peter Behrens, who is considered to be the first "corporate designer." In 1907, Behrens was appointed "artistic advisor" to the Berlin-based business AEG and used the filament bulb idea in his first advertisement. On the Chloé dress, the bulb appliqué even has the customary pointed tip, while the leg-of-mutton sleeves suggest a rounded bulb. The bulb idea came to life as Andrée Putman, an interior designer, entered a party at Le Palace nightclub wearing the dress.

Another important factor in Lagerfeld's success was his aptitude for marketing. He frequently took the Concorde to New York to go to "trunk shows" there. These private displays gained popularity throughout the 1970s and got their name from the typical method of shipping clothes to their destination in trunks. According to Rosemarie Le Gallais, Lagerfeld received the kind of welcome typically given "to a head of state" when he landed in Houston in May 1979 to debut his autumn collection for Chloé. Lagerfeld was driven into the city in a vehicle with enormous longhorn steer horns on the hood as a purple carpet was extended by the jet, a crowd of cheerleaders lined the streets, and a police convoy followed. At the Neiman Marcus department store fashion presentation, he was treated like a star and he liked it.

There were certain clear distinctions between Lagerfeld and Jacques Lenoir despite their increasing success. While his designer was incredibly giving, the managing director was naturally conscious of his finances. Renate Zatsch, a former model for Chloé, recalls Karl yelling, "Run!" and pushing the girls to flee, augmenting their paltry earnings with the Chloé outfit they had worn for the event. Without changing, the models hurriedly escaped through the back door.

Some underlying resentments were also fueled by the designer's rising prominence. When the first Chloé fragrance debuted in 1975, Lagerfeld rose to fame and wealth. For the Elizabeth Arden perfume contract, Lagerfeld and Chloé had established a new business called Karl Lagerfeld Productions, with the shares to be split three ways. Gaby and Jacques each received 25% of the shares, and Lagerfeld received 50%. Even after Lagerfeld left, Chloé kept making new fragrances. However, he was the driving force behind the introduction and worked closely with Elizabeth Arden on the product and the bottle for many months. In 1977, the scent brought in more than $20 million in revenue, and Lagerfeld is said to have gotten 2.5% of that total. This amounted to half a million dollars for that year alone, which was a large sum of money for the time and continued to rise as the perfume's sales soared dramatically. Aside from his numerous other occupations, he was also very well paid for his work as a fashion designer at Chloé.

After Lagerfeld left Chloé, female creative directors predominated at the design house that specialized in feminine clothing. He added, in response to the hiring of Stella McCartney, "I knew they would take a big name to replace me at Chloé, but I thought it would be in fashion and not in music." The London designer was unfazed by this and explained that her mother Linda had purchased several Chloé dresses made by her predecessor in the 1970s. Following Phoebe Philo's four-year tenure at Chloé, Paulo Melim Andersson in 2006, Hannah MacGibbon in 2008, Clare Waight Keller in 2011, Natacha Ramsay-Levi in 2017, and Gabriela Hearst in 2020 took over for Stella McCartney. The fact that there are so many distinct names demonstrates that nowadays, top football teams switch managers almost as frequently as fashion houses do with their designers. The company was able to consistently update its image by adding new designers to its roster.

Long before she passed away in 2014 at the age of 93, Gaby Aghion sold her stock in the fashion firm at the opportune time. Philippe Aghion, her son, pursued a career in economics with a focus on growth models while keeping his mother's expanding company in mind. The label is still friendly with the descendants of its founder; Philippe Aghion's daughter Mikhaela occasionally works there. To Karl Lagerfeld's great credit, Chloé continues to be one of the most significant brands on the ready-to-wear calendar. He was the designer who stayed at Chloé the longest of all—for a total of 25 years—after elevating the company to global recognition in the 1970s.

They kept the Fendi sisters waiting. No one answered the doorbell at the flat when they visited Paris in 1964 to persuade Karl Lagerfeld to sign a document committing them to working together. The sisters did the only thing they could: they simply waited for him to show up while sitting in the hallway. In Paris, the hallway lights go off after a minute, so they took turns standing up to turn the lights back on. "Now it's your turn!""Now, off you go!""Now it is your turn!" Three hours later than expected, their new business partner arrived. Silvia Fendi recalls how her mother, aunts, and mother-in-law frequently recounted the incident while laughing. He was frequently late.

Rome was a frequent destination for Lagerfeld, especially in the early years of his collaboration with Fendi. In those days, he even possessed an apartment in the middle of the city. But after joining Chanel in 1982, his visits became less frequent, so he chose to stay at the Hotel Hassler, which was close to the Palazzo Fendi. From 1965 until his death, he served as the company's artistic director, setting a record for a fashion industry employee. He frequently traveled to Milan for the Fendi ready-to-wear shows and flew out to Rome hundreds of times. He also sent agents from Paris to Rome to see how business was doing because he always wanted to keep everything under control. His close friends Gilles Dufour, Hervé Léger, Vincent Darré, Eric Wright, and Amanda Harlech all went out to the Italian capital one after the other to make sure that things weren't taking an eternity even if they were in the Eternal City. Ideas were exchanged by phone and fax almost daily between Rome and Paris.

Even though he wasn't directly in charge of the brand's accessories, Lagerfeld had an impact on Fendi bags as well. Silvia Fendi observed Lagerfeld and her mother at work when she was a young child and was inspired by their techniques. She experimented with bags in the same way that they did with furs and gowns, launching the "It" bag era in 1997 with the "Baguette." This famous handbag's name was a pun that combined the English word "bag" with the French diminutive form "-ette."

The Fendi atelier resembled a laboratory more than a creative space. A young designer with bleached blond hair and bulky chains was on the accessories team at the time. The designer who Lagerfeld dubbed "DJ" because he was usually blasting music loudly was actually named Alessandro Michele, and starting in 2015, he would have immense success as Gucci's creative director. Pierpaolo Piccioli and Maria Grazia Chiuri were two other innovators who contributed to the creation of the "Baguette". When the former maestro retired, they both joined Valentino and took over as co-creative directors. Maria Grazia Chiuri ultimately succeeded to the position of Dior's first female creative director. Three of the most significant fashion designers of the early twenty-first century—Michele, Chiuri, and

Piccioli—all learnt from Karl Lagerfeld how to bring ideas to life and how to maintain their inner freedom in the face of the many demands the fashion industry placed on them.

Fendi's bags, the global "logomania" movement, and the distinctive business signets all contributed to the brand's popularity in the 1990s. A welcome boost came from the Baguette bag's inclusion in the television program Sex and the City. When luxury goods behemoth LVMH began to gradually buy the business in 1999, the quick expansion at Fendi accelerated. Lagerfeld has a cordial relationship with LVMH CEO Bernard Arnault, who frequently sent him the newest Louis Vuitton goods. Arnault was thrilled with the significant purchase because it demonstrated to Chanel that he had a claim on Lagerfeld as well. Additionally, it demonstrated to rival company Kering—which was the owner of Gucci and Bottega Veneta—that LVMH was also succeeding in Italy. The somewhat possessive attitude of Arnault was happily noted by Lagerfeld. Lagerfeld was obviously not going to produce a good trophy, but he also wasn't going to upset Arnault either.

When Bernard Arnault entered the picture, Lagerfeld was confident that he could advance things, just as he had done at Chanel. His dreams came true when Fendi staged a massive, symbolic ready-to-wear parade near the Great Wall of China in October 2007, seizing an entire market by demonstrating respect for its culture. Numerous Chinese models walked the runway to commence the show, donning attire in the auspicious hue of red, and the enormous boundary wall was sensationally illuminated.

The Fendi 90th anniversary presentation in July 2016 was equally rich in Rome-related symbolism: the models crossed the Trevi Fountain's water like Jesus did on the Sea of Galilee, although on a plexiglass platform. Then, at the start of July 2019, the brand held a significant couture display on the Palatine, one of Rome's seven hills, directly across from the Colosseum, as a tribute to the designer. The brand revealed fifty-four looks—one for each of Lagerfeld's fifty-four years with Fendi—amid the ruins of the old Roman city. This view of their city was a favorite of the ancient Roman emperors, and the Emperor of Fashion would have appreciated it too.

Even in the most unlikely places, Karl Lagerfeld remnants can be discovered. Between Bologna and Milan in the southern Po Valley, Reggio Emilia is an unexpected treasure trove of this man's creations. His sketches have been preserved from the effects of time here, in the frigid Max Mara archives. Even though the sketches are more than 50 years old, they almost appear to have just been created yesterday. On a yellow folder that Lagerfeld delivered in the year 1971 from Paris to the regional capital in northern Italy, the words "Max Mara—Eté 72" are written in his handwriting.

The founding father of Max Mara, Achille Maramotti (1927-2005), and Lagerfeld conversed in French. He signs off, "Cher Monsieur." "All the explanations are on the sketches," His sketches for summer 1972, which are incredibly precise, are a direct result of this designer's rigorous training in the haute couture school. A semicircular cape without linings (cape demi-cercle non doublée) has an exact radius of 110 cm. A fabric sample and the color-specific notation "en rouge étrusque" are both included with a sketch of a jacket. The designs also feature a pair of two-tone shoes, which is an intriguing prelude to Lagerfeld's work at Chanel, where Coco Chanel created her iconic beige pumps with black toe caps in 1957. A bolero jacket is supposed to be trimmed to allow for "toute la liberté du mouvement," according to the directions. This demand for a lot of mobility nearly seems like the idea for building a liberated woman, totally free from fashion restrictions.

Business in Lagerfeld's native Germany increased as a result of the success he was establishing for himself as a successful German in Paris. He began working with Fritz Ertelt, a businessman in the fashion industry from Selm, a town close to Dortmund, in 1969. Ertelt frequently took flights to Paris to peruse the designer's designs and select the ones he liked the best. Lagerfeld then had the prototypes produced in his atelier and shipped them to Ertelt in Selm. And that's how Parisian style entered the collection, according to Ulla Ertelt, the businessman's daughter. However, she adds, "people talked about who was behind the Saint Mignar line behind closed doors, which also contributed to the success." The company was not permitted to use Lagerfeld's name for commercial purposes. During her time as an intern at Chloé from 1979 to 1981, Ulla Ertelt also learned to understand Lagerfeld's distinctive blend of optimism and impatience. "Karl possessed an unstoppable creative energy. Working for one label alone would never be sufficient for him. Additionally, as the son of a Hamburg businessman, he was aware of how to maximize advantageous licensing agreements.

In 1975, Willebert Boveleth, a businessman from Mönchengladbach in North Rhine-Westphalia, approached Lagerfeld in an effort to establish a collaboration that would help advance his enterprise. After decades of success in high-end fashion, Wibor Textilwerke, founded in 1950, sought to launch a line with a well-known designer to commemorate its 25th anniversary. A licensing arrangement for the "Karl Lagerfeld Impression" line was made after Boveleth looked up Lagerfeld after it had been recommended by the German trade publication Textilwirtschaft. The designer travelled to Düsseldorf each month with his helper Rosemarie Le Gallais to draw the collection. The Boveleths' home, where the housekeeper served the sauerbraten he so adored, was where they always went after being picked up from the airport and transported to the Mönchengladbach office for the fittings. He would occasionally take a siesta after lunch before returning with Rosemarie to the fittings to board a flight back to Paris that same evening.

However, Lagerfeld quickly continued on his way. With the release of the Chloé fragrance in 1975, his notoriety reached new heights, and with numerous new deals in the works, he was traveling to Japan for business considerably more regularly. He sold the Bidermann Group his trademark rights in 1984, two years after joining Chanel. After the American company started working to go through the maze of licenses he had created for himself, the designer finally cut ties with Wibor. The distribution of the new collection "KL—Karl Lagerfeld" for the German-speaking world was temporarily taken over by Willebert Boveleth's son Peter, who was now a member of the Wibor board. Beginning in 1988, Karl Lagerfeld collaborated with Klaus Steilmann, who oversaw the largest apparel manufacturer in Europe at the time. The "KL—by Karl Lagerfeld" line was even marketed in the Quelle German catalog from 1996 to 1999.

At the start of the 1970s, everything seemed to be going well. Karl Lagerfeld was an expert in both the business and design aspects of the fashion industry. In addition to the enormous inheritance he had received from the death of his father, he had established himself at Chloé and was earning sizable amounts from all of his side businesses. Early in 1968, Elisabeth Lagerfeld transitioned from being a frequent visitor to a mainstay at his spacious apartment at 35 Rue de l'Université after the purchases of the family residences in Baden-Baden and Hamburg were finalized. The designer's personal life benefited from all the professional and financial independence he had established for himself. The gregarious, giving character gained a ton of new acquaintances when he unhurriedly celebrated his achievements. After the upheaval of May 1968, France exuded a sense of social emancipation, which brightened his life even though he wasn't really sure why protests were taking place directly outside his door at the Sorbonne and in the neighborhood.

The newcomer excitedly greeted Lagerfeld. The 1960s fashion pattern of straight lines and slightly boxy proportions was gradually giving way to more sensual lines, and he could sense a shift in the fashion industry. The entire vocabulary of fashion was evolving and becoming more flexible. Lopez joined Chloé without hesitation thanks to Lagerfeld, who asked him to assist on the brand's advertising motifs and sketch the newest ideas. According to designer Tan Giudicelli, who worked at Chloé in the 1960s, "He came with that New York energy." He had a great impact on the Chloé brand. He had been taken by Karl, and Antonio needed Karl as well. The kind German offered Antonio and his partner, fellow Nuyorican Juan Ramos, shelter in an apartment close to his own house.

Antonio, in Karl's opinion, embodied the full stylistic freedom of the free artist. But he had other American personas besides Antonio. Additionally, he got along well with Juan Ramos and was impressed by his methodical approach to gathering novel concepts, fashions, and artifacts. Juan and Karl frequently visited La Hune to buy books on fashion, design, and art. Juan would also buy movie posters, artwork, postcards, and other finds at flea markets if he believed they may inspire whatever project Antonio was working on at the time.

He served as the art director and ongoing inspiration for his boyfriend. Karl picked up on his "magpie-like approach" and began accumulating ideas for the concept of each new collection as part of his preparations.

Elisabeth Lagerfeld also visited with Karl's acquaintances. Tippin remembers, "One evening, I unlocked a door in Karl's enormous apartment—and she was seated there. I said, "Excuse me," and after talking for a while, it became clear that she recognized me: "You're Corey, aren't you?" The elderly woman was friendly and obviously aware of Karl's social life. The entire gang traveled to Saint-Tropez in the summer of 1970, where Lagerfeld frequently vacationed with Anne-Marie Muoz and her family. The lovely home that Karl had rented out housed Corey, Donna, Antonio, Juan, Karl, and Mrs. Lagerfeld. The fact that a 73-year-old was present when the Americans were on vacation struck them as odd. According to Tippin, "Our interactions with her were very proper." "We were laughing in class like schoolchildren, behind the teacher's back. I wish we had been a little bit more responsible. We didn't sit there graciously after dinner; instead, we leapt up and left.

Even Karl, a new buddy of Antonio's, began to relax a little. Karl began donning tunics or silk pants from Chloé at Saint-Tropez, but his mother continued to support Sonia Rykiel since she didn't want to overly flatter her son by donning his creations. Pictures of the group at the beach show a man who is very different from the rather reticent fashion watcher that people were used to seeing. Antonio carried a Kodak Instamatic 100 that allowed him to take candid photos of his pals rather than a conventional camera, which could have made his subjects uneasy. His photographs show a man lounging in the sun, a handsome young man in sunglasses resting his elbows on a Coca-Cola box like he's in a commercial and holding a bottle in one hand as if he's about to sip from the straw, and a muscular man in a one-piece bathing suit sitting by the Mediterranean Sea with wet hair and a playful expression of annoyance while pointing at the photographer.

Only Antonio was the recipient of Karl's unabashedly sensuous side show. Karl met Antonio in New York in 1976 after he had relocated there, and Antonio was still willing to participate. The images from the "Men in Showers" series depict middle-aged Karl putting on a playful sensual performance with the shower's water stream. The water nearly appears to be gushing from his mouth, like some kind bearded water fountain. He can be seen in the shower sporting a sizable pair of sunglasses in the last row of images. In his own contribution, he manages to maintain an ironic distance from any references to the sadomasochistic and fetishistic elements of Lopez's Instamatic series. However, not everyone displayed such shyness in front of the camera. It is incredible how many young, attractive people Lopez's art has made famous. Along with Jerry Hall, another muse living at the Hôtel Crystal, he also assisted in the development of the careers of singer Grace Jones and actress Patti D'Arbanville, Cat Stevens' ex-girlfriend and the subject of his 1970 hit song "Lady D'Arbanville." He also made the acquaintance of Tina Chow, a fashion icon who wed Michael Chow, the creator of the hip Mr. Chow restaurants, in 1972, and Jessica Lange, who went on to appear in King Kong and receive Academy Awards for her performances in Tootsie and Blue Sky.

Only Karl was hesitant to benefit from "gay liberation" in any way. He avoided getting involved in the mischief and kept most people at a safe distance. His hesitation was pretty natural given that his sexually active buddies were a good ten years younger than he was, as well as the fact that he had a decent number of job obligations. The other members of the group had less responsibilities and worked independently. In the end, Rosemarie Le Gallais describes him as a "grand solitaire who was happiest working from home." Still, if nothing else, his clothes began to reflect this newly discovered sexuality.

Karl felt compelled to fit in and partake in the scene, if only to prove to the scene-setters that he had his own group of friends, much like Yves Saint Laurent, who was never seen without his entourage. The changing role of the fashion designer went hand in hand with the seductive attraction of these two men and their love of drama. Designers had never been celebrities before the 1960s; they were merely service suppliers. But upper-class society began to take fashion houses like Yves Saint Laurent, Valentino, Lagerfeld, and

Halston in New York. Why? since they were wealthy. They signed their names to scents and received rewards beyond their wildest expectations, which was the main source of their newfound income. And with all that money, they were able to purchase luxurious residences with exquisite interior design and ever-growing art collections.

In October 1970, Andy Warhol traveled to Paris in search of ideas and with the intention of making a movie. This experimental artist, who was caught in the crossfire of two opposing clans, was in for an interesting few months. On one side was Yves Saint Laurent and his group, and on the other was Karl Lagerfeld, who was accompanied by all the young, attractive people Andy was already familiar with from the US. The pop artist needed to be on the German designer's side and not in Saint Laurent's sphere of influence. Maybe that was one of the reasons he agreed to let the movie crew use his apartment on Rue de l'Université.

Fred Hughes, Warhol's business partner, accompanied him from the Factory in New York, and when they arrived in Paris, he was introduced to the city's high society. Paul Morrissey, a filmmaker with whom Warhol had collaborated on several of his avant-garde films since 1965, also joined them. Their new movie—originally titled Gold Diggers '71, Les Beautés, or Les Pissotières de Paris—was about two American ladies who came to Paris in search of the ideal wealthy man who might help them achieve their goals. One of these women was Donna Jordan, who had just been found and had lately been featured in a Guy Bourdin photograph that appeared on the cover of French Vogue; the portrait even appears in one of the movie's scenes. Jane Forth, who had previously portrayed the major role in Warhol's film Trash, served as her co-star. Forth began her career as a receptionist at the Factory. Because Andy admired Corey Grant Tippin and convinced him to join the project as a makeup artist, he was in charge of the actors' physical metamorphosis in the movie. Karl Lagerfeld was cast as a German aristocrat, one of the wealthy, youthful, heterosexual men.

Later, Lagerfeld had fewer than glowing things to say about the entire affair. He declared, "It was the most immature filmmaking ever." Although he was able to perform in such a manner in his youth, he subsequently admitted, "Today, I wouldn't play anyone other than myself." To make the kissing sequence less embarrassing, he made light of it. However, there's another way to look at it: "It was such an outrageous scene," adds Tippin. "I'd never seen Karl kiss anyone before, and now here he was all of a sudden with this intensity." The kissing scenario also shows that Karl could only display closeness in public if they were artistic, childish, or both.

If two Frenchmen hadn't stepped in, Karl's extended American family's fun times may have continued indefinitely. In addition, Karl's adversary Yves Saint Laurent's entourage was frequently rubbing shoulders with Karl's group in Paris, almost as if they were dependent on one another to exist. Karl had begun meeting Jacques de Bascher in 1972. The Americans eventually became aware of the changes taking place.

The evening spent in Pierre Bergé and Yves Saint Laurent's residence was very vibrant. Omar Sharif, the star of Lawrence of Arabia (1962) and Doctor Zhivago (1965), took opium alongside actor Helmut Berger, who had gained notoriety in Luchino Visconti's The Damned in 1969. In one of the rooms, a television was playing pornography. Fueled by drugs and drink, some of the visitors chased Saint Laurent's dog around the flat. Thadée Klossowski de Rola and other French guests felt the Americans were thrilling. He noted in his fragmented journal: "Tippin and the women around Antonio Lopez and Karl, a little court / dazzling beauties / not ungraceful / fantastic dancers."

The spotlight was constantly on Saint Laurent. He took on the role of representing Parisian fashion after the passing of Elsa Schiaparelli in 1973 and Cristóbal Balenciaga in 1972. The brand-new duplex apartment he and his roommate had been residing in since 1972 at 55 Rue de Babylone featured a sizable garden and was a residence befitting of a head of state. Karl Lagerfeld, who could see that his enduring adversary was stepping up his game, of course didn't show that he was worried by all of this. And as his American pals drew farther away from their German friend in Paris, the more they became closer to Saint Laurent's world.

By this time, Jacques de Bascher had come into Karl's life and was letting everyone know about it. "He came to Saint-Tropez one day in the summer of 1972," claims Corey Grant Tippin. He was a relatively young man who was still getting a handle on Karl's world. He was irritating and attracted a lot of Karl's attention. Jacques lacked style. He wore formal clothing, as if he were a student at a prestigious boarding school or a fraternity member. Even his fashion sense seemed strange to them. The Frenchman frequently discussed his noble ancestry and was obviously proud of them. He studied our attire and imitated it. He wasn't even considered handsome by the Americans. What then, did the elder Frenchmen find so alluring about Jacques, who had turned twenty-one that summer? "As gay men, they felt less guilty being with Jacques: He came from a good background, and he wasn't just some gigolo you could pick up at a urinal," claims Tippin. "For Karl, Jacques was like a brand-new project. He was someone you could bring to any dinner party because he was intelligent, young, and well-groomed.

In the heat of Saint-Tropez, Lagerfeld's bond with the Americans rapidly waned. In 1972, Juan Ramos began seeing the painter Paul Caranicas, and Karl detested his new love interest. According to Caranicas, "He was envious of my relationship with Juan and he was furious that Juan and Antonio were gradually drifting away from him." He, on the other hand, believed the fashion designer to be pretentious and annoying: "Karl was very insecure and envious of other people's talents. For instance, whenever we discussed my work, he only had negative things to say.

The setting for this friendship-cum-rivalry was Le Sept. While Karl's family made some memorable appearances at the nightclub, frequently making a beeline for the disco, Yves dined upstairs with his idols Loulou de la Falaise and Betty Catroux, not forgetting the rather sour-faced Pierre Bergé. Karl Lagerfeld, the voyeur, watched as Donna Jordan, the pale star with a gap between her teeth, danced naked on the table, and Renate Zatsch, the slim Rhine beauty, reveled in her newfound freedom. The newest visitor, a long-legged Texan with flowing blond hair, fell for Antonio Lopez's attractions. She quickly became the current fashion model after Jerry Hall fell head over heels for her. During a fashion shoot for British Vogue in Jamaica in 1975 with photographer Norman Parkinson and stylist Grace Coddington, the couple became engaged. Nevertheless, it was short-lived, as Jerry Hall quickly moved on, first to Bryan Ferry and then to Mick Jagger.

Just a few weeks before Antonio, on February 22, 1987, Andy Warhol passed away in New York. Complications from a routine gall bladder operation led to his demise. Warhol had taught Lagerfeld that having a distinctive appearance may make one become an icon and that artist collectives are capable of coming up with brilliant ideas. In the middle of the 1970s, Wolfgang Joop met his fellow countryman, Karl Lagerfeld. "Karl Lagerfeld reminded me of Andy Warhol," he recalls. Isn't it true that both of them surrounded themselves with a group of individuals who could partake in all of life's excesses for them while they protected themselves like their own bodyguards? Their inventiveness depended on their sobriety. Their work won praise and respect from the obvious, the surface-level, even the "impersonal." Any similarities to the pop star were always dismissed by Lagerfeld. He aspired to originality. In 2007, he stated, "First of all, I'm better groomed." "And he also shoved people. Never do I press individuals.

In the early 1970s, he first encountered Karl Lagerfeld at La Coupole. When the fashion designer entered the Montparnasse brasserie with a group of friends that included Antonio, Juan, Donna, Pat, Eija, and Kenzo, the young Japanese designer who soon rose to fame on the Paris fashion scene, the young Frenchman was already seated in the establishment. Later, Jacques recounted how La Coupole as a whole experienced a "divine silence" as the group entered.Karl was the star of the show. Even back then, he exuded confidence. According to Alicia Drake, "Jacques saw a group of people living the life he yearned for in that suspended moment."

School didn't appeal to Jacques. From the Lycée Pasteur in Neuilly, he changed to the Lycée Janson de Sailly in the sixteenth arrondissement of Paris. Later, he enrolled at the Lycée Charlemagne in the Marais, which had previously been attended by writers like Honoré de Balzac and Victor Hugo. He struggled with the lecturers in a number of disciplines. Historiography: "He draws attention to himself, but sadly not through his work." He is acting in an "unacceptable" manner. Math "is respectful and idle."

This was the turning point in this bon vivant's lifestyle. Jacques was accompanied by Lagerfeld, who dubbed him "Jako," to his favorite tailors, Cifonelli and Caraceni, where he placed an order for custom suits and shirts. The designer later remarked, "We wanted to wear garments that no one else possessed, shirts printed with my designs. And Jacques now toured the streets in Lagerfeld's Rolls-Royce or his Bentley rather than his family's Citroen 2CV. They began to be referred to as "les Lagerfeld" by Thadée Klossowski de Rola in his journal. The two guys went out together and enjoyed the open, easy talk, regaling each other with ideas, anecdotes, and rumors, but they didn't actually get married. The relationship would last for around seventeen years.

Many of Jacques's adventures went unnoticed by Karl, or at least that was the impression he left. According to Wolfgang Joop, "He took things in stride and loved that mischievous child." He described having someone around as "impossible," and he felt it was amazing. The fact that the designer's partner had extramarital affairs didn't appear to concern him. However, things changed when Jacques and a female friend began stopping outside schools while driving about Paris in Jacques' Rolls-Royce, enticing boys to join them in the back, and then luring them with champagne and other temptations. Philippe Heurtault, a friend of De Bascher, recalled Lagerfeld's response after learning the truth: "I'm not paying anymore." Jacques once called Karl a sell boche (filthy German), but they could also be incredibly rude with one another. "Jacques loved the money, but it was like living in a gilded cage," claims Heurtault. And he was limited to what Karl gave him, which wasn't always what he desired.

Karl didn't like it either when Jacques tried to seduce ladies. However, this Don Juan smashed down all barriers of gender, age, and shame since he relished the conquest at least as much as the deed itself. To him, it was similar to a drug. When Yves Saint Laurent entered the picture, things only became trickier. The relationship was starting to lose its shine at this time because the fashion designer had been working with Pierre Bergé on both a professional and personal level for so long. Saint Laurent became a hero in the gay community after Jeanloup Sieff's photos of him in a naked state for Pour Homme, his first eau de toilette for men, went viral. The young aristocratic dandy who was already working with Lagerfeld was the target of this timid-appearing but incredibly tenacious designer. Maybe that contributed to the attractiveness.

In little time at all, Jacques was residing in Karl's former flat at 6 Place Saint-Sulpice like a king. The Saint-Sulpice Church, which was also built in the seventeenth century and had towering windows overlooking it, was visible. Because Lagerfeld's mother was dissatisfied with the flat on Rue de l'Université, he moved to the picturesque square. He wasn't particularly fond of it either since he believed it was cursed—not by Andy Warhol's misguided movie, but by an apparition. Karl claimed that a woman's spirit who used to reside there kept showing up to Karl's cousin Tita's daughter. She would apparently be sitting in the kitchen at the end of the corridor or strolling along it. He subsequently stated, "Everyone who lived there after me died in mysterious circumstances."

On the other hand, the large apartment in Place Saint-Sulpice didn't appear to be a haunted place. Here, Lagerfeld was given even more latitude to indulge his love of art nouveau, and starting in 1973, he started to furnish the home with objects of art and furniture from the 1920s. However, he soon outgrew this fascination as well, and his passion for the eighteenth century led him back to Rue de l'Université. This time, he moved into the townhouse at number 51, Pozzo di Borgo. Now, Jacques engaged in some questionable actions in the Place Saint-Sulpice residence. He gave a celebration in 1976 in honor of Jean-Claude Poulet-Dachary, a former member of the French National Front and the Foreign Legion. A Harley Davidson Sportster 1200 was located in the center of the space. After an accident, the designer who had purchased it for Jacques decided to forbid him from using it. Jacques changed the mirrors so they were pointing upward, heaped cocaine on top, and left some razorblades and straws on the glass so that people could assist themselves because he had nowhere else to put the Harley.

Yves and Jacques dissolved their relationship in 1975, maybe as a result of Karl Lagerfeld's involvement, Pierre Bergé's unrelenting rage, Yves Saint Laurent's submissive demeanor, Jacques de Bascher's thirst for adventure, or any combination of these factors.

In the 1970s, Paris and New York were the ideal locations for people looking for total independence. When Karl and Jacques arrived in New York via plane, Studio 54 was always their first trip. Early in the night, the designer would return to The Pierre hotel on Fifth Avenue, while Jacques continued the celebration in a number of seedy clubs. Rosemarie Le Gallais recalled rushing out of her suite to meet with Lagerfeld for the first appointment of the day, then running into Jacques on his way home after one of these nocturnal excursions.

The catastrophic prognosis for Jacques de Bascher was given in 1984. At first, he kept it to himself and just told his partner, but it quickly became evident how helpless he had become. He withdrew and endured the therapies. Karl spent a lot of time with his girlfriend despite his aversion to illnesses, protracted illnesses, and passing away. The designer purchased Le Mée, a home in Le Mée-sur-Seine, close to Fontainebleau, in 1985. Karl and Jacques were both supposed to heal in this location. However, Jacques was brought to the Raymond-Poincaré hospital in Garches, west of Paris, in 1988. "Karl visited him every day," claims his assistant Eric Wright. On a spare bed in his hospital room, Lagerfeld slept throughout his partner's final four nights. On September 3, 1989, Karl was present at Jacques de Bascher's death.

Even during those trying times, he maintained his strength. "It didn't take him long to get back into the office," recalls Caroline Lebar, Lagerfeld's longtime assistant. He exercised strict discipline. He didn't lack any feelings; rather, he merely decided not to express them out of respect for others. Pierre was cremated. His ashes were divided in accordance with his last will and testament; one urn was given to his mother and the other to his life partner. Years later, Lagerfeld claimed he was keeping it—along with his mother's ashes—in a vault. "Someday, my ashes will also be buried there."

A fortuitous meeting like the one he had with Jacques, according to Lagerfeld, only occurs "once in a lifetime." After Jacques left, he wasn't searching for a "second-rate replacement." "The same thing should never happen again and cannot."

Two friends were standing in the elevator of the 12-story skyscraper on the upscale Avenue Montaigne in 1973, directly across from the Hotel Plaza Athénée. They were Helmut Newton and Karl Lagerfeld, and at this time, they were well acquainted. Both men had the rare qualities for professionals in the fashion industry—humor, sharp wit, and cheek. Knowing that no one else could comprehend their jokes, they laughed while cracking German gags.

Newton and Lagerfeld were en route to a brief adventure. Marlene Dietrich, a fellow Berliner, was going to be introduced to Newton at last. Their common acquaintance, a native of Hamburg, was anxious to introduce the entrepreneur photographer to Germany's biggest diva since he loved bringing people in his life together. In the elevator that led us to Marlene's flat, "he was like an excited schoolboy," Lagerfeld remarked. It seems that the actress had a significant impact on Newton's sexual development when he was a young boy in Berlin. And there she was, welcoming her visitors in person. She appeared stunning in Lagerfeld's opinion. It was unfortunate that the meeting between these three well-known Germans had to go apart so dramatically.

Rarely has one person assimilated German culture with such vigor. Karl Lagerfeld loved German literature and watched a lot of German movies, especially the classics. He loved all German music, from Richard Strauss to Lotte Lenya and Kraftwerk, and was particularly intrigued with designers and architects like Peter Behrens and Konstantin Grcic. He authored complete books on German literature, cultural history, and photography, and was frequently seen reading German periodicals and newspapers. He produced graphics for newspapers, worked as a photographer for publications like Stern and German Vogue, knew a number of editors and artistic directors, as well as actors like Veronica Ferres, Marie Bäumer, and Diane Kruger.

He discovered who he was as a German in Paris. When he was still very young, he had left his native country behind. He also didn't crave for home much while he was just getting started in his new life, like many young people who leave their homes to work or study abroad. He spent the 1950s settling down in France, and the 1960s were spent establishing his career. But as he grew older, he became more conscious of his ancestry. He once declared, "I am completely German." And he no longer felt humiliated by it: He instantly sent Carine Roitfeld, the editor-in-chief of Vogue, a collection of Hildegard Knef CDs after learning that her father liked the singer. Knowledge breeds confidence. Lagerfeld frequently collaborated with Germans, and he adored every facet of German culture, including its ostentatious side: He did, in fact, pose in front of a silver-tinsel-draped Christmas tree in the 1980s.

Many of the designer's German obsessions were personified in Marlene Dietrich. The Berlin-born actress, who gained international recognition after appearing in The Blue Angel (1930), became one of the few German stars in Hollywood. She was born in 1901. She may have lost some of her elegance over the years, but Lagerfeld was still drawn to Dietrich's effortless Berlin wit, razor-sharp wit, and easygoing style: "She only ever wears jeans and men's shirts," he observed in 1973, "but sometimes I bring her an old pajama-style mock-up from Chloé."

Even then, Dietrich was lost in her own thoughts. She was obliged to relocate into a less expensive flat with views at the back from her former property in Paris, which looked out onto a posh avenue. She nevertheless shared many traits with Lagerfeld. "Things were the same for Karl Lagerfeld as they were for Marlene Dietrich: They had both outgrown Germany," recalls Princess Gloria von Thurn und Taxis, who was able to understand this situation. Germany was not big enough for them. Even Paris was becoming too small for this diva at this point. Lagerfeld was asked to take over when French Vogue chose to print a special edition honoring her in December 1973. He displayed to her a selection of images taken by each of the photographers Vogue was considering. Dietrich had to choose who she wanted to hire to take the pictures because the magazine needed fresh shots. Guy Bourdin was passed over by Dietrich, who told

Lagerfeld, "I'd like to meet him." In agreement, Lagerfeld offered to have him over at a later time.

Karl Lagerfeld, the unfortunate middleman, thought it was all too much and that he no longer wanted much to do with Dietrich. He nevertheless kept sporting the present she had previously given him: a gold Cartier pin dating back to 1937. Peter Bermbach claims that "Karl only had negative things to say about her." "He cut off communication with her." He could no longer picture her as the refined woman she previously was at that point. The geraniums outside her window and the pigeons she was constantly attempting to scare away with a water pistol were topics this lady spoke about far too often. She quickly isolated herself completely. The former actress, who was now experiencing muscle atrophy, spent her final years at home and kept no one from looking at her. Everything about this woman's private life remained a secret, shrouding her existence. She gave Lagerfeld a lesson as a farewell present before she passed away in 1992. He was quite fascinated with the idea that discretion was practically a myth, which she had taught him.

On January 23, 2004, Helmut Newton passed away. He was oddly close to the woman he had dreamed of as a little boy. By the oddest of coincidences, Marlene Dietrich's burial and the photographer's tomb are both located in the Friedhof Stubenrauchstraße cemetery in Berlin-Friedenau. When Lagerfeld learned that his old acquaintance had indeed been buried there in 2004, he was shocked. Dietrich and Newton had not gotten along when they were alive, and now they would have to live together for all of eternity. He expressed outrage and said that his friend had been buried in the incorrect spot.

It wasn't the first time that his response was a little excessive. June Newton, the widow of the photographer, had nothing against the two well-known Germans being interred close together. Particularly since it was about half a mile to the home at 24 Innsbrucker Strasse, where the young Helmut Neustädter was born and raised before he immigrated and became Helmut Newton.

Even in the afterlife, these three German legends couldn't seem to get away from one another. Through fashion, Lagerfeld used his own unique method to reestablish contact with the German diva. After his passing, many of the models walked the runway in Marlene pants for his final ready-to-wear collection, which was unveiled in March 2019.

In July 1975, Wolfgang Joop and his wife Karin visited the area for Haute Couture Week. He drew the graphics and she wrote the content for a collection they had already worked on in Germany, but they were in Paris on assignment for the national Sunday newspaper Welt am Sonntag. They believed that Yves Saint Laurent was the creator of the universe. Even so, that didn't lessen their excitement when they unexpectedly ran across Karl Lagerfeld and his group on the street one day. The Joops, who were about thirty years old, stood out because they were dressed bizarrely by German norms. They started talking after Lagerfeld inquired about their identities, and they got along right away. They were asked to spend the weekend at the château in Brittany that Lagerfeld, a man of swift judgment, had just acquired.

The older couple and the established designer had a lot in common, especially when it came to their shared passion for old Prussia. As his visitors sat across from him at the château supper table, Lagerfeld drew sketches of them. He replied, turning to face Wolfgang, "I'm drawing a Prussian squire with a cigarette." Lagerfeld discussed Menzel's Round Table and his childhood desire to own the artwork in these aristocratic settings. What a coincidence: When visiting his aunt Ulla in the Bornstedt neighborhood of Potsdam, the young Wolfgang frequently roamed around the expansive park at Sanssouci Palace.

Lagerfeld had relocated to 51 Rue de l'Université, a 10,750 square foot apartment back in Paris. He was free to indulge his passion for the eighteenth century both here in his new country château and in the structure that once housed the Pozzo di Borgo hotel on the Left Bank. He viewed the pre-revolutionary France's exuberance as a welcome counterpoint to the repulsive modernism that ruled the art and architectural worlds in the 1970s. It was also ideal for Jacques de Bascher, whose counterrevolutionary ancestry and outlandish clothing perfectly reflected the time.

Lagerfeld must have been delighted that the château was in desperate need of refurbishment as he was eager to go deeper into the eighteenth century. The garden was overgrown, the outbuilding was crumbling, and the château itself was in bad shape. The designer got to work on his latest endeavor, researching historical texts, browsing auction catalogs, speaking with specialists, and creating plans. According to his friend Patrick Hourcade, Louis-Nicolas Van Blarenberghe drew heavily on the bed room and gallery hall of the Hôtel de Crozat on Rue de Richelieu in Paris, which were immortalized in one of the famous snuff boxes in circa 1770. Like he loved the eighteenth century, Lagerfeld liked miniature painting. He continued to spend the better part of twenty-five years immersed in the period, continuing his earlier preoccupation with art nouveau, until the turn of the new millennium, when he made the decision to leave the past behind him and live entirely in the future.

Lagerfeld was successful in revitalizing the château. The entire area was bursting into bloom. Vogue contributor Anna Piaggi, who became one of Lagerfeld's idols because of her unusual style and flower-adorned hats, was a frequent guest. Before emerging in the most ridiculous of ensembles, the Italian fashion writer spent hours getting ready, which of course required Lagerfeld to sketch. When Lagerfeld's pals visited the area, the residents had a hard time believing their eyes. For instance, Jacques went out for coffee in Grand-Champ while wearing a white suit and a Panama hat, and numerous visitors were noticed walking around the neighborhood park in vintage silk jackets. At times, people even confused the lord of the manor with Demis Roussos, a well-known Greek musician who, like Lagerfeld, had dark hair and a bushy beard.

On Sunday, the Joops boarded a train headed back to Paris with Lagerfeld and bid their new acquaintance farewell at the station. Lagerfeld couldn't stay for very long because he had to leave to continue working on his Chloé collection before the holiday shopping season started in August. Brittany experienced tragedy in a few weeks. José was accused of being in charge of the accounts when some money went missing from Grand-Champ. The twenty-eight-year-old made an effort to refute it, but Lagerfeld was unmoved. José jumped beneath a train close to Vannes on August 26, 1975. His death was attributed to the train that Karl and Jacques had taken at Vannes on their way back to Paris, according to the locals. The young man had actually flung himself under the train that was moving the other way.

Over the years, Joop and Lagerfeld traded scathing criticism and cutting remarks in the media. In a 2011 interview, Lagerfeld intended to say one or two more derogatory things about Joop: "His drama is that he's not me. He is unknown on a global scale. He can mimic anything rather well, but he lacks his own sense of flair. Although it wasn't true, the hypothesis was intriguing. Through his Wunderkind label, Joop had long since developed his own distinctive look, drawing inspiration in part from Prussia.

At Château de Penhot, the Prussian mystique persisted, especially after Elisabeth moved there. She had traveled from Germany to Paris in the spring of 1968 to be with her son, and now, perhaps more than ever, they were close. In Bissenmoor and Hamburg, nannies frequently took care of the kids, but after relocating to France, Elisabeth stayed close to Karl. Karl had only ever shared a residence with her. She was sitting on the sofa reading the German press when Antonio Lopez apparently felt forced to draw her because he thought she was so fascinating to look at. It was a close bond between a mother and son. Because she formerly wore a large woolen coat and because the Americans thought the name sounded funny, Karl affectionately called her Wollmaus (wool mouse). Elisabeth's joy in her son is evident in a letter she wrote to her sister in 1972, despite the caustic tone: "The crazy youngster has merely gone and grown himself a beard. Imagine! On him, the hair does indeed grow quickly. Grandpa looks like he might have climbed out of the picture frame.

Karl was quite busy and couldn't take care of his mother by himself. In a letter to her sister during the summer of 1969, Elisabeth stated, "He is irrepressible when it comes to work, like his father." Who was she meant to turn to for companionship when she was stuck at home during the day with a member of the staff and barely knew anyone in Paris? Renate Zatsch, a model who occasionally worked for Karl, dropped by for a visit and said, "She was happy when I came to visit, because I'm German like her." In addition, Peter Bermbach made a few trips to see the elderly woman at Lagerfeld's request. "I discussed Germany, the weather, or her son with her." However, he made every effort to avoid seeing her in public because "she wore a turban and dressed like a circus princess." The cultural writer found her dress to be out of character. German women used to conceal their hair with turbans when their hairdressers were gone at war. However, nobody would have been caught dead in a turban at four in the afternoon in 1960s Paris. People were reminded of the discredited actress Arletty when they heard about it since she had a connection with a German air force officer during the occupation and was labeled a collaboratrice after the war.

Elisabeth experienced a chronic cold in the late summer of 1978, more than two years after the stroke that had negatively impacted her health. Before the doctor was scheduled to arrive to prescribe cold medicine on Thursday, September 14, she scheduled an appointment for her hairdresser to visit the château that morning. The well-groomed 81-year-old passed on that day, right as the doctor arrived.

When Jacques died in 1989, the meaning of Château de Penhoet was lost to Lagerfeld. Even though he owned the château for at least 15 years, the designer insisted that he never returned. In June 1990, he did make one final special appearance when he invited an English royal guest into his little Sanssouci. The lord of the manor and his honored guest, the Queen Mother, enjoyed tea in the garden while admiring the lovely flowers on display. They also stood next to a table with a massive pyramid of colorful macarons perched on top of a white tablecloth. However, this would essentially be a farewell visit. In the 1990s, Lagerfeld sold the mansion and had most of the furnishings transported to Pozzo di Borgo and his getaway in Le Mée-sur-Seine. He also paid off the tax debts he had acquired over the years with the money he made from the activity that had been his favorite pastime in the 1970s.

In December 1980, Ettore Sottsass, Matteo Thun, Michele De Lucchi, and a number of other designers created The Memphis Group. The group was named after the ancient Egyptian capital and

Tennessee, the state where Elvis Presley was born, and like the late singer, these designers weren't afraid to shake things up. These designs broke the rule that form should follow function, with their erratic lines, strange shapes, and vivid hues that could make a Bauhaus enthusiast like Karl Lagerfeld cry.

Lagerfeld, who is constantly innovative, was enthused by what he saw. He undoubtedly foresaw the beginning of a new postmodern age or, at the very least, a departure from minimalism in the 1980s. The fact that the designer had discovered the ideal furniture for his new residence in Monte Carlo made him delighted as well. He later said that he had never lived in a modern building before and had no idea how to decorate it. Memphis was just what he needed, and he really did want it all.

In addition, Lagerfeld used the 1991 Sotheby's auction to sell many pieces of furniture and decorative objects from his collection of art deco. The Vase de tristesse (about 1900) by ceramicist Émile Gallé sold for the highest price at an auction with a bid of 550,000 francs from a Japanese buyer. For 340,000 francs, the Centre Pompidou acquired seven significant pieces of Eileen Gray furniture from her E-1027 property in Roquebrune, including a Transat chair made of wood and synthetic leather that dates to around 1929. The E-1027 table, which was expected to fetch no more than 60,000 francs, was bought by a private German museum for 160,000.

Karl Lagerfeld was a man who made rash decisions and acted on impulse. This included the furnishings and interior decor he chose. "I'm a fashion person," he said. "I switch up my wardrobe, furniture, homes, and collection. Change is a part of life. When things reach a point where improvement is impossible, you change. For him, making this sacrifice wasn't a big deal because "I have no sense of possession." The interior designer took the same attitude to his furnishings as he does to new projects and discarding old ones. His assistants, the employees of the moving companies, the packers of furniture, and the warehouse staff would not get any sleep. Even after settling on a particular look, Lagerfeld had the parts moved around between Paris, Grand-Champ, Monaco, Le Mée, Hamburg,

Biarritz, and warehouses until the picture was finished—and started to get boring to him.

In Paris, Lagerfeld heightened his enthusiasm for the eighteenth century to an entirely new level. His passion for the period, which was first sparked when he first saw the Menzel painting as a child, was now manifested in a sizable collection that kept expanding. He remembered the Louis XVI chest of drawers and a pair of gilded French Régence chairs that had been restored in yellow suede and had taken pride of place by the windows of the ground-floor apartment he had occupied on the Quai Voltaire in the early 1960s as his first purchases. It is probable that Lagerfeld didn't get the Régence chairs until much later because his old friend Peter Bermbach cannot recall seeing them in the flat. Perhaps the designer simply imagined the chairs returning to the apartment. Whatever the case, it is obvious how significant this type of furniture was to him.

The potential for transformation was one benefit of having so many residences. New apartments provided fresh backdrops for photoshoots, filming, and interviews. For his film L'Amour, Andy Warhol shot at the first apartment on Rue de l'Université. Stéphane Audran starred in a Chloé perfume commercial that was filmed on Lagerfeld's Place Saint-Sulpice property. Anouk Aimée also made an appearance there in the 1978 movie Mon premier amour. The ideal location for photo shoots was the iconic Monte Carlo estate La Vigie, often known as "the lookout tower" in Monaco. This three-story cuboidal mansion, which was first constructed in 1902 for British publishing mogul William Ingram, sits on a hill and has a sizable terrace with sweeping views. One of Lagerfeld's friends, Prince Rainier III, offered him the property on the condition that he restore it after it had been vacant for a while. Lagerfeld reportedly contributed $14 million to the idea and agreed. The reception hall on the ground level was converted into a dance floor and a photographic studio, and the villa was refurbished and furnished. For his private accommodations, Lagerfeld selected the top floor, where one of the baths faced west for views of Monte Carlo at night and the other faced east for dawn vistas of the Mediterranean. La Vigie hosted a variety of events over the course of a decade, including shoots, parties, and product launches. In the end, there were no longer any opportunities to explore, and the villa's mission had been fulfilled.

The designer was still living in his Monaco penthouse and has been working on Villa Jako in Hamburg since 1991. Then there was Villa Elhorria, his new refuge in Biarritz, which he had been furnishing with decor from the 1920s and 1930s, including ceramics, lighting fixtures, and furniture. On May 15, 2003, he sold off the massive amount of modernist pieces he had amassed over the years for his residences in Biarritz and Monaco at Sotheby's auction in Paris. There were more than 200 things advertised, the most prominent of which were the roughly 50 pieces of furniture designed by Frenchman Jean-Michel Frank. The choices of works by Pierre Legrain, Marcel Coard, Eileen Gray, and Paul Dupré-Lafon further demonstrated Lagerfeld's exquisite judgment. The art deco pieces from the 1920s and 1930s included pottery by Henri Simmen, lighting by Maison Desny, a chrome inkwell by Émile-Jacques Ruhlmann, and a lavish mirror by Dagobert Peche. A little under 7 million euros were raised.

His 2008 purchase of a property on an island in Lake Champlain seems to have been rather impulsive. Perhaps, in contrast to the futuristic setting of his new residence on the Quai Voltaire, he regarded this Vermont property as a chance to express his internal conflicts in questions of taste. This designer loved development, but he also loved the naivete of Grandma Moses's art and the idyllic depiction of American life in Norman Rockwell's paintings. He paid $500,000 on the Vermont home without giving it a second thought. Although he never lived there and only occasionally visited, the purchase was profitable nonetheless: it served as the setting for the Chanel spring 2009 ad campaign and finally served as a pretty significant gift for one of his favorite models, Brad Kroenig.

When it came to his interiors, Lagerfeld kept things simple. The twentieth century has come to an end, according to him. His vast collection of artifacts from the eighteenth century was largely gone. The eight-room flat at 17 Quai Voltaire was transformed into an ultra-modern environment, with the library hidden behind two sets of twenty-five retractable glass doors on either side and the rooms divided by glass panels rather than walls. With the push of a button, both doors simultaneously opened to show Lagerfeld's extensive library of reading and art books. In 2005, when he first came into this flat, his entire outlook on life was forward-looking. Except for himself and all the books, he didn't want any reminders of the 20th century here.

The architect would have lunch in a different apartment, one of the numerous he owned and rented nearby and frequently visited for lunch, to read the paper, or to host visitors. Even though he didn't use them since they were "too tiny" for him, he preserved the furniture from his boyhood room. A stunning set of Biedermeier furniture was present. He had learned to write and draw at this desk as a young boy, and his mother had placed paintings from his room on the wall "because they weren't good enough for her." He called these German Romantic paintings his mother's "leftovers," although he never offered them for sale.

Chapter 3:
Brilliant Career (1983 to 1999)

He had plenty of time to launch his own clothing line. Since 1961, Yves Saint Laurent and Pierre Bergé have achieved enormous success using the name of the French fashion designer. Karl Lagerfeld famously stated, "In Hamburg, unlike in Oran, nothing is less elegant than displaying your name over the door. I could have followed closely behind them. A shopkeeper cannot be both an industrialist and a lender. He stated in 1987: "I can still remember the sarcastic remarks they used to make about Hamburg merchants who ran businesses." He went on to explain that his parents would not have been eager to lend their name to a fashion house. The responsibilities didn't exactly excite him either. Who wants to place orders, cost materials, or manage staff? He preferred to work for other labels so that if something went wrong, it wouldn't be his responsibility. Furthermore, as his former coworker Rosemarie Le Gallais puts it, "A fashion designer who doesn't have to deal with the business side of things is freer and possibly a better designer as a result."

The two socialist presidents of France, François Mitterrand (1981–95) and François Hollande (2012–17), shared Lagerfeld's dislike of hypocrisy. He appreciated the republican Nicolas Sarkozy (2007–12), the neo-Gaullist Jacques Chirac (1995–2002), and the president elected in 2017 Emmanuel Macron, who avoided the left–right paradigm in his politics. Lagerfeld's positive interactions with each president's spouses were a sign of his regard for them. Bernadette Chirac wore his clothes, and she frequently attended his fashion presentations. Carla Bruni-Sarkozy was a familiar face to him from her modeling days, and she frequently sat in the front row at his Chanel shows. Small-group dinners allowed him to get to know the Macrons better, and he didn't think Brigitte Macron looked bad because she wore Louis Vuitton most of the time.

The specter of socialism had the gorgeous rich and beautiful affluent people of Paris shaking in their boots in the spring of 1981. They were apprehensive that a government led by Mitterrand would cause France to shift toward the East, their wealth, and its future political alignment in the Cold War. Many of these people sold their shares and withdrew their money out of the banks, which led to a 30% decline in stock prices.7 Fearing a tax increase, Helmut Newton relocated to Monaco and persuaded his friend Karl to do the same. Lagerfeld registered as a resident of the principality in the summer of 1981 since he was acquainted with the royal family and already had two flats, one for Jacques de Bascher and the other for himself, on the twenty-first floor of the Millefiori building. He routinely flew to Monaco in the beginning, spending entire weekends there, and he maintained his official residency there up until his passing. However, even this was ultimately unable to stave off the Parisian tax authorities.

On the Paris Fashion Week ready-to-wear agenda, things started to pick up speed. It was the height of Christian Lacroix, Thierry Mugler, Claude Montana, and Jean Paul Gaultier's careers. Issey Miyake, Yohji Yamamoto, and his girlfriend Rei Kawakubo (creator of Comme des Garçons), who intrigued Lagerfeld with their moody designs, followed in the footsteps of the Japanese innovator Kenzo. One young businessperson seized an opening when it presented itself. After finishing his engineering degree, Bernard Arnault joined his father's construction business. In 1985, he bought the failing textile firm Boussac Saint-Frères, which owned Christian Dior. The billionaire made a purchase of Christian Lacroix two years later. The French firm LVMH (Mot Hennessy—Louis Vuitton) then made him the main stakeholder in 1989. Along with Louis Vuitton handbags, Mot & Chandon champagne, and Hennessy cognac, LVMH already produced a wide range of high-end goods, such as fragrances, cosmetics, watches, and other wines and spirits. In the years to come, even more well-known names would be added to the list. A long list of fashion brands, including Givenchy, Céline, Berluti, Kenzo, Loewe, Fendi, Emilio Pucci, and Loro Piana, will soon join Arnault's kingdom, where the sun never sets. In the 1990s, his adversary François-Henri Pinault was also among the first to see the possibilities for fashion in the luxury goods industry. He made an investment in the expanding industry by acquiring fashion businesses for his company, which was renamed Kering in 2013, including Gucci, Yves Saint Laurent, and Bottega Veneta.

As a frequent visitor to the United States while working at Chloé, Lagerfeld was no stranger to the country. The highest sales were made in the US, where he had a perfume arrangement with Elizabeth Arden. They now had one additional reason to travel, as Jacques also enjoyed taking flights to New York. Lagerfeld routinely took Concorde flights, frequently with Rosemarie Le Gallais and occasionally with his partner, and he always had a dozen or more suitcases with him. Less than three hours were spent on the flight. This hypersonic vehicle was the ideal representation of a hypersonic designer. That doesn't mean he always showed up on time, though.

"One time we were all on the plane with the engine running," Rosemarie Le Gallais recalls, "and we had to wait another quarter of an hour for him to turn up."

For Chanel, the eponymous label served as a trial ground for new ideas. Ideas were exchanged back and forth in Paris. In addition, Lagerfeld found plenty of inspiration from his side jobs, such as the time he spent creating the costumes for the Salzburg Festival performance of Hugo von Hofmannsthals play Der Schwierige (The Difficult Gentleman) in the summer of 1991. Eric Wright discovered a transparent skin-colored stretch fabric at the Munich fabric trade show while looking for materials for the costumes. They used a slightly modified version for the Karl Lagerfeld collection because he and Lagerfeld liked it so much.

According to Gaubert, who already knew Lagerfeld from Le Palace, "We were made for each other." He was frequently seen in the store, had a crazy record habit, and was very knowledgeable about music. He purchased every new item. He was interested in what additional information was available because he was familiar with the old information. In the fall of 1989, the fashion designer called Gaubert into his office, gave him a copy of Malcolm McLaren's most recent album House of the Blue Danube, and asked him if he could do anything with it. Gaubert immediately teamed up with DJ Dimitri from Paris and got to work. Instead of adding new songs one after the other, they made a continuous soundtrack: "We blended soul with house, Bizet with soul, and Pavarotti with house. It was a crazy mash-up of styles. And after the fashion show, everyone in the audience wanted to know who composed the music.

The compassion of Lagerfeld included his belief in other individuals. This attitude was immensely inspiring to his team, and his ability to delegate efficiently was made possible by his trust in others. In the same way that his father had used a strategy based on division of labor to oversee hundreds of workers at several places before him, Karl was now doing the same. This strategy needs a careful balancing act between oversight and trust. In order to free himself up to concentrate on his sketches, he had to give up management of the fittings and entrust them to Virginie Viard, Eric Wright, and his most devoted director of atelier, Anita Briey. They would be in the atelier for the morning fittings while he was working on sketches at home for a different collection. Modern workplaces are very specialized, which suited Lagerfeld because he was adept at surrounding himself with the right people for the proper jobs. He had a huge amount of work capacity and little patience for discussions, complaints, or meetings. He was a highly effective communicator who gave detailed directions.

A few hundred feet from Place de la Concorde, where Marie Antoinette was executed on October 16, 1793, the Lagerfeld team was in the studio on Place de la Madeleine for fittings one day in September 1993. The group was developing a line of clothing inspired by the former French queen. Each person in attendance was depicted by Lagerfeld in a photograph on paper while sporting a Marie Antoinette wig. He drew a hand carrying Céline Toledano's decapitated head by her shock of hair when it was his turn. The sword of Damocles had been drawn, in the manner of the eighteenth century.

At the Karl Lagerfeld line, things were becoming even more challenging. The designer was unable to concentrate on his own firm with the same zeal since he had so many assignments to manage. Ralph Toledano, his managing director, felt underappreciated since he now had to answer to Mounir Moufarrige, the CEO of Chloé. After a while, a disgruntled Toledano left the label, following his wife Céline, who had done so a year before. Since 1996, the fashion house has been losing money. Lagerfeld received the trademark rights to his own brand back from Richemont after his contract with Chloé expired in 1997. However, the Johann Rupert-founded Swiss organization made the decision to retain Chloé.

Up to this time, effective partnerships between fashion designers and their managers had been exemplified by Yves Saint Laurent and Pierre Bergé, Tom Ford and Domenico De Sole, Marc Jacobs and Robert Duffy, and Alessandro Michele and Marco Bizzarri. Now that he could, Lagerfeld joined them. Ralph Toledano had a good tenure with him in the 1980s, and now he had at last discovered the ideal managing director once more: Righi claims, "We have a sizable collection here. It serves as a special storehouse for us. Since 2006, every design has been captured on camera, preserved, and properly kept away. Hun Kim, the design director who joined Karl Lagerfeld in 2015, is familiar with fashion rules. "Our logo is a silhouette," he claims. There is no other brand that uses a head silhouette as its trademark; other companies have polo players or crocodiles.

Much like Coco Chanel, Christian Dior, or Yves Saint Laurent, Karl Lagerfeld continues to influence fashion through his business. However, unlike high-end ready-to-wear or haute couture collections, these costs are not outrageous: This brand has more logos, is less prestigious, is younger, and is considerably more reasonably priced. At Karl Lagerfeld, where a motorcycle jacket costs 795 euros, a trench coat costs 495 euros, a pinstripe tunic costs 195 euros, and a T-shirt costs 89 euros, the profit margins are lower. The products and brand image are targeted at a younger demographic than the rest of the luxury market, with a large social media following and clients between the ages of 25 and 35. Carine Roitfeld, a former editor-in-chief of French Vogue, and Sébastien Jondeau, Lagerfeld's bodyguard and confidant, are all prepared to continue revitalizing the name as brand ambassadors.

Karl Lagerfeld's headhunting resembled a covert expedition. The head of Chanel's US department, Kitty D'Alessio, had been following the fashion designer for a while. She adored his dexterity and enjoyed his Chloé collections. She made sure there were flowers and presents from her ready for Lagerfeld when he checked into The Pierre in New York. Rosemarie Le Gallais explains, "She tried everything she could to seduce him." And it succeeded.

By this time, Lagerfeld was aware of his value and was not going to be a simple target. The negotiations began in secrecy since Lagerfeld couldn't risk being caught entering the Chanel headquarters in Paris on sight. He was invited to a meal with Alain Wertheimer in London in 1982. Rosemarie Le Gallais flew with the fashion designer, Kitty D'Alessio, from Paris. Wertheimer and Lagerfeld clicked right away. Le Gallais notes that, despite their affluence, Alain and his brother Gérard Wertheimer are amicable and down to earth. They complemented Karl well.

Karl Lagerfeld was drawn to Coco Chanel because she was more than just a pioneer in fashion. She was an inspiration to him since she stood up for herself and refused to be pushed around by guys. She also had a loose tongue. When he started to thoroughly research the designer's life and work in 1982, he was undoubtedly reminded of his mother. From the countryside as well, Elisabeth Bahlmann—who had passed away only a few years earlier—had left for the big city when she was a young lady. Additionally, she had worked in 1920s fashion firms and advocated for women's rights, just like Coco. For Lagerfeld, working at Chanel was akin to completing some sort of biographical task. Elisabeth, who was 14 years Coco Chanel's junior, had given up her job as a manager in Berlin. A legend who resembled her as much as one Chanel suit does the next was now represented by her son, who was working in his mother's honor. Lagerfeld's mother shared many traits with the renowned fashion designer, including her short hair, sardonic look, biting wit, and strong feminist ambition.

The younger Karl used to make fun of the conservative dressing of this older woman. During a late 1950s brunch at the Ritz with his friend Victoire Doutreleau, the topic of Coco Chanel came up. The designer resided in one of the suites at The Ritz until her passing, and it was conveniently adjacent to the Chanel corporate offices. She must detest the word "sexy," don't you think? The designer scoffed. He made a sarcastic remark that was representative of the time. Due to her dislike of miniskirts and jeans and her inability to adapt to the times, Coco Chanel had lost the public's favor. Her style no longer accurately represented youth. As Lagerfeld later penned in the preface to a book of pictures by Douglas Kirkland, this put her "in the position of the has-been oracle of style and fashion" and would render the years to come "clouded for her by gloom and bitterness."

When Coco Chanel passed away in 1971, the fashion house was being run somewhat shoddily. The couture collections were taken over by Yvonne Dudel and Jean Cazaubon, two of the designer's old aides. Marietta Andreae, who worked for the company from 1976 to 1980 as director of public relations for Germany and Austria, claims that "but they croaked under the pressure." At this time, Chanel No 5, arguably the most well-known perfume in the world, provided the majority of the profits. In their gilded chairs, the audience members at the shows in Rue Cambon remained securely seated. Andreae recalls seeing the Chanel suit in burgundy with a dark blue trim one time and dark blue with a burgundy trim the next. During her time as a junior editor at French Vogue in the 1970s, Sophie de Langlade recalls her editorial office colleagues' lack of excitement for the company. "Who's going to Chanel?" would be the question of the season. The writers would all agree to respond, "Moi non!"

Chanel's modernization effort was started by Lagerfeld on January 25, 1983. His new collection, his first as the company's creative director, was unveiled to the fashion house's visitors, including Isabelle Adjani, Paloma Picasso, Claude Pompidou, Andrée Putman, and the others. The models appeared in contemporary, well-tailored gowns with striking proportions and deep, full pleats. The traditional beige and pastel colors were replaced by contrasts, which included a lot of red, white, black, and blue. Similar to Coco's return in 1954, the reception to Lagerfeld's debut haute couture line for Chanel was muted. But things quickly turned around: "The success started with my second season," he acknowledged.

The level of Lagerfeld's mastery increased. He was extremely seasoned yet still had a lot of drive, and his versatility showed through in a wide variety of styles. His ideas literally spilled out of him. He arranged the ateliers, successfully delegated, struck deals with financiers, and was successful in picking the interest of his clients. Since Yves Saint Laurent's debut at Dior in 1958, nothing like it had ever been seen in the fashion industry. Here, Lagerfeld was using entirely other aspects to disrupt the founder's recognizable aesthetic. This type of deceit, which simultaneously satirizes and reveres the tradition, called for tremendous confidence.

At Chanel, some disputes stretched on for years. Karl Lagerfeld and Jacques Helleu, two of Alain Wertheimer's most experienced creatives, were to collaborate at the company. The son of Coco Chanel's friend and artist Jean Helleu, the artistic director was in charge of coordinating the look of the perfumes, cosmetics, watches, and fine jewelry. However, Wertheimer's concept was never carried out. Evidently, Helleu was envious of his colleague's success. According to Lagerfeld's publisher Gerhard Steidl, the designer once compared the gap between Chanel's fashion and perfume divisions to the Berlin Wall, only wider. Frances Stein, the accessories designer for Chanel, needed to be held accountable, according to Lagerfeld. With a play on Frances Stein, he gave her one of his humorous catchphrases, "Frankenstein."

Lagerfeld had extremely high standards for both himself and his coworkers. He was eager to act and inflict his vengeance on anyone who didn't measure up. He was sensitive to people, and Madame Colette was one of them. She was in charge of sewing the delicate fabrics, draperies, and garments at the haute couture flou atelier. She committed a grave error involving Christy Turlington and Linda Evangelista while working on the haute couture show in July 1990. These two models would rule the modeling world for the following decade after appearing on Peter Lindbergh's renowned British Vogue cover with Naomi Campbell, Tatjana Patitz, and Cindy Crawford in January 1990. The front flaps of Christy and Linda's redingotes were undone when they stepped onto the runway, revealing more than just their matching thigh-high boots. The models' underwear was visible to the entire audience. Natasha Fraser-Cavassoni, who served as his assistant at the time, claims that Karl "was fit to be tied." The sight amused others, including Caroline of Monaco, a friend of Lagerfeld's. The designer, however, had no patience and ordered Madame Colette to go immediately.

This designer simply wanted to see things in a different light; he wasn't aiming to alter the environment. Lagerfeld was commended for his chameleon-like ability to adapt to the Chanel aesthetic and make it work for him by German fashion journalist Antonia Hilke. This man became a sort of reincarnation of Coco Chanel's spirit by immersing himself in her world and giving her style a new life. Like Coco Chanel, who transformed her early poverty into a privileged childhood, he likewise fabricated some aspects of his life story.

But Lagerfeld persisted in adjusting and evolving. Lagerfeld didn't ignore the trend when designers like Thierry Mugler and Gianni Versace began including overtly sexual themes in their clothing in the 1990s. For the spring/summer 1994 show, he wore Naomi Campbell in a miniskirt that was barely there, and for the autumn/winter 1995 show, he had Stella Tennant walk the runway in a micro-bikini top with just a strap holding her nipples in place. However, not all of Lagerfeld's bold looks were successful. When Claudia Schiffer debuted on the runway for the spring/summer 1994 show in a haute couture gown with a form-fitting bustier that had verses from the Koran embroidered on it, a media frenzy ensued. In his mistaken assumption that it was an Indian love poem, Lagerfeld had stolen the material from a book about the Taj Mahal.

Even Karl Lagerfeld found the expansion of the market for luxury products to be astounding: "There are so many new markets, and there are so many new stores in China. The US market appears to be getting smaller by the day. Chanel began investing its outstanding profits in specialized shops like jewelers and shoemakers.By 2019, the Paraffection division of Chanel was home to 27 artisanal companies, also referred to as maisons or ateliers d'art. When workshop proprietors are getting senior or the fear of closure hangs over the company, Chanel steps in: Bruno Pavlovsky, managing director of Chanel's fashion division and a close collaborator of Lagerfeld for almost three decades, adds, "We have to protect their savoir-faire." Given that the majority of maisons are found in or close to Paris, maintaining them is even more crucial. "Deliveries must be made quickly because we have a collection scheduled for six weeks. We need our suppliers close by, and we need to be able to continue doing business with them in 20 years.

Lagerfeld drew inspiration from the craft workshops for his Métiers d'Art concept in 2012. In order to honor the masons and their labor, Chanel began releasing a brand-new, carefully designed line of apparel in a different location every year, taking advantage of a lull in the fashion calendar before Christmas. Lagerfeld was already juggling two ready-to-wear presentations and the corresponding pre-collections, as well as two haute couture shows, before the additional show was added to his list of responsibilities. For consumers who traveled to warmer climates during Christmas starting in 1990, he also had the Chanel cruise collection to present in May. The last two lines were introduced by Lagerfeld in 2018: Coco Neige, a line of down coats, ski pants, and boots for skiing vacations, and Cocoa Beach, a line of swimwear, beach bags, espadrilles, and other products for retailers in seaside towns like Saint-Tropez. At Chanel alone, there were eventually eleven annual collections to plan. And he developed all the concepts for them.

As the workload increased, Lagerfeld's helper began to assume a larger and larger responsibility. Virginie Viard began her career as an intern at Chanel in 1987 and then worked for Lagerfeld at Chloé from 1992 to 1997. Her maternal ancestors had been Lyon-based silk makers. Upon returning to Chanel, the French designer focused solely on haute couture before finally adding ready-to-wear to her duties in 2000. She was in charge of translating and explaining Lagerfeld's sketches to the chief seamstresses in the ateliers, known as premières, in her capacity as studio director. The team would work on the designs all day until Lagerfeld arrived for the two hours of fittings in the late afternoon or evening. It was a well-organized, productive process. In the studio, hierarchy had no place. Despite how forthcoming he was, his mode of operation was clear. "I can do whatever I want, however I want," he declared. Although I have a direct line of communication with Chanel's president, he never orders me to do anything. It is not subject to debate.64 He was expressing his goals clearly by making statements like this. He was relegating the management of the fashion house to the background in a way that no other designer in the new millennium would ever dare. It also worked out well since Bruno Pavlovsky always had the discretion to keep a low profile: Even concepts that may have originated with the president were credited to the renowned creative director.

Lagerfeld claimed, "I do it all: design, image, advertising, retail. "At Fendi, it's less clear-cut. Large corporations are full of little bosses. Bernard Arnault, the owner of Fendi, was told by me that I could make the brand more Chanel-like, but they would have to put up with my practically dictatorial working practices. Since I pause and consider my words before I speak, there are no inconsistencies with me. That does not mean that I cannot alter my viewpoint. However, I don't seem to alter my viewpoint all that frequently.

The brand's fragrances, cosmetics, watches, and jewelry benefited from the fashion division's continual expansion. With all the fashion shows, advertisements, commercials, and store openings, Chanel was gaining visibility. However, with so many other roles to play on other stages, this star actor was careful not to overshadow the fashion company itself. Lagerfeld's celebrity also contributed to raising the label's image. Despite the fact that Lagerfeld adored his job at the company, he insisted on maintaining a safe distance.

Chanel reported group sales growth of 12.5% to 9.88 billion euros and net profit growth of 16.4% to 1.9 billion euros on June 17, 2019. In 2018, the business released its operational data for the first time. Patricia Riekel said in her tribute to Lagerfeld that he had his own notion about what would happen to Chanel after his passing: "Chanel will probably be sold to the Chinese," he predicted. In Paris, where Chanel had essentially become a part of the national cultural legacy, this prediction was not warmly received.

The celebration was tranquil; the celebratory atmosphere of the evening satisfied any urges for takeovers. How long, though, would Bernard Arnault be able to restrain himself from this alluring possibility? He rose to third richest man in the world just before the homage, and a year later he paid nearly $16 billion to purchase the Tiffany & Co. jewelry company in the United States. The Wertheimers are completely aware that this individual has more riches. Karl Lagerfeld gave Chanel the reputation of being untouchable, and they will need to maintain this reputation for some time to come.

It all started with shoddy photos for a Chanel press package. In the 1980s, it was impossible to find major photographers for jobs like these, therefore quality always deteriorated. Eric Pfrunder, Chanel's image director, was informed of Lagerfeld's complaint and challenged him to see if he could improve upon it. "Okay, now you do it," Pfrunder said. There was no need to ask Lagerfeld twice. He took it upon himself to do all of the photography for Chanel's press kits beginning with the spring/summer haute couture collection for 1987. After that, he photographed the haute couture line for the 1987 fall/winter season, and soon he was responsible for all of Chanel's fashion campaign photos.

Lagerfeld's side business grew in significance. Soon, his work moved beyond stock photos and advertising campaigns and began to explore the fields of abstract photography, fashion photography, and portraiture. Over the years, he wrote books, displayed his work, and developed as a photographer. He never achieved the same breathtaking heights as a photographer that he had as a fashion designer, of course. He made up for this, though, with his passion for composition, his tireless pursuit of excellence, and his enormous amount of labor. Gerhard Steidl provides the following account of the occasionally tense experience of working with Lagerfeld: He claims that he began taking pictures at nine in the evening and that he realized he needed to make further adjustments at three in the morning. Model Julia Stegner recalls the exhausting late-night shoots in Rome, where they persisted "until the stylist eventually said she had no more outfits." As she and Lagerfeld were seeing the results on the TV together, he invited her to "come here, Julia, and sit on my lap!" If that had come from anyone else, it might have sounded strange, but not Lagerfeld. According to Stegner, "He had this really paternal way about him."

A significant photo shoot requires a lot of diverse components to work together successfully. This much is evident in the Modern Mythology series, where Lagerfeld attempted to meticulously recreate the mood of Longus's Ancient Greek romance Daphnis and Chloe. He had come across the well-known pastoral story in a 1935 printing with drawings by German artist Renée Sintenis. When creating the stage directions, Lagerfeld first copied the drawings: "It was an exact script, and he spent weeks preparing it," says Steidl, who also worked on the picture shoots.

It didn't take Lagerfeld long to choose Baptiste Giabiconi and Bianca Balti, two of his go-to models at the time, to play the story's foundlings. Filming started in Saint-Tropez in 2013 after the romance's backdrop was hastily changed from Ancient Greece to the South of France. In his Rolls-Royce that summer, Lagerfeld led the convoy of stylists, hairdressers, makeup artists, and photographers, who were being transported by a number of black vans. Following closely after them were two vans carrying food and beverages, followed by the animal trucks carrying goats, lambs, horses, and a cow. Last but not least, there were the furniture trailers that had sculptures scattered over the woods seemingly at random. It took three days to accomplish the entire task. On the set, there were also a few cooks, a butler, and waiters. There was afternoon coffee and cake, and they put up folding tables in the woods and covered them with white tablecloths.

For Lagerfeld, images by themselves were not always sufficient. Various outfits from Chanel's history were photographed on mannequins for the exhibition catalog as part of the setup for a major Chanel show at New York's Metropolitan Museum in 2005. According to Gerhard Steidl, who collaborated with Lagerfeld on the idea, "the dresses didn't hang right." He absolutely disliked the way they seemed. Following the creation of large-format copies of the original pictures by Steidl, Lagerfeld cut out the clothes and assembled it into collages. Following that, Steidl produced a second print of the pictures, which Lagerfeld tinted with lipstick. He searched through 1920s fashion magazines for the right pictures, cut off the heads, placed them over the bodies, and had another print printed. The layered drawings were then converted into a series of algraphy prints using a unique technique. The "Channel Then Now" project had an astounding budget, but the end product was a piece of art.

Toward the end of his life, Lagerfeld also organized photos. His selection for the 2017 Paris Photo exhibition attests to his knowledge with great photographers like André Kertész and Lee Friedlander, as well as the abstract architectural works of Mathieu Bernard-Reymond and Mat Hennek. Two works by Swiss police photographer Arnold Odermatt, who spent decades capturing accidents, were also selected in the collection. This selection is intriguing from a biographical perspective: One of the pictures shows a Mercedes that looks to have wound itself around a pole after a collision, evoking Lagerfeld's personal experience in the 1960s.

His passion for photography also inspired him to pursue movies. Starting with a handheld camera and subsequently switching to his iPhone, he began shooting short films on picture shoots. The Return, a 2013 short film featuring Geraldine Chaplin as Coco Chanel returning to Paris in 1954, was one of his most serious cinematic ventures. Reincarnation, a short film from 2014, was likely the pinnacle of his cinematic innovation. Cara Delevingne plays the Austrian Empress Elisabeth ("Sisi") and a hotel maid in the film, and Pharrell Williams plays Franz Joseph I and the elevator guy who served as the model for the enduring Chanel jacket. While on vacation in Salzburg, Geraldine Chaplin reprises her role as Coco Chanel, who is inspired to apply the notion of the jacket for women's fashion after spotting the elevator attendant's uniform. Such a concept could only have been thought of by Karl Lagerfeld. perhaps Coco Chanel. or either.

When it came to finding models, Lagerfeld was more nimble than others. Inès de la Fressange, who was born in 1957 and signed an exclusive deal with Chanel in 1983, was a person he got along with very well. The model, who is simply referred to as "Inès" in France, played a crucial role in boosting the brand's recognition. The face of Chanel was reportedly paid 650,000 marks ($270,000) a year from the outset, according to German fashion journalist Antonia Hilke. But she also made a sizable profit for the business in addition to earning a large sum for herself. She was a brand ambassador before that was even a job title, and a supermodel before that was a thing.

Everything was going smoothly until 1989, when Inès sat for the Marianne bust, a representation of the French Republic. It did not impress Lagerfeld. He considered everything to be bourgeois, offensive, and local. He retorted, "I do not dress monuments. Inès then broke off contact with Chanel. Everything happened quickly: She was absent from the runway lineup as early as the haute couture show in July 1989. Their breakup was a bombshell that sent lips buzzing for weeks in France. Although Lagerfeld later provided a different explanation, the real cause of the controversy was never revealed: "One day she embarrassed M. Wertheimer by demanding for more money in front of other people. Therefore, he instructed me to "Invent something to get rid of her." Marianne was a figment of my imagination, and I couldn't give a damn.

In the 1990s, Schiffer and Lagerfeld produced more than any other designer-model team the world had ever seen. On the runway for Chanel, Schiffer logged plenty of miles, she has featured in more Chanel ad campaigns than any other model to date, and she frequently went on the Concorde to New York with Lagerfeld to support him at events. More than a thousand magazine covers featuring Schiffer throughout the years have been captured by Lagerfeld, who also wrote books about her. His images of her appeared on the covers of trend publications including Self Service and Vogue. "Karl was a wizard," claims Schiffer. "He made me into a supermodel from this shy German girl," I said. He taught me everything I know about style and fashion, as well as how to make it in this industry. She even attracted the French, who described her as the reincarnation of a young Brigitte Bardot. She also assisted Chanel in capturing entirely new markets with her flawless image. Even the fashion shifted with Claudia, according to Sophie de Langlade, a Chanel employee at the time. She was attractive, and the collections mirrored her attractiveness.

When it came to securing the models he desired, Lagerfeld was also powerful. He was the creative director of three, occasionally four fashion firms, and he knew how to make the most of his clout. He made a subliminal threat: "Ah, what a shame, then she won't be able to model at Chanel or Fendi either." If an agency refused to offer a model for one of the Karl Lagerfeld shows, for example, if another label had first refusal. He ensured he always had access to the hottest models by using his power in this manner. "And it wasn't just the models," adds Eric Wright. The same procedure was done by him with fabric makers.

The models for Lagerfeld, who served as brand ambassadors, gave the designer access to entirely new realms. Vanessa Paradis, Claudia Schiffer, Stella Tennant, Kristen McMenamy, Devon Aoki, Cara Delevingne, Lily-Rose Depp of Vanessa Paradis, and Kaia Gerber of Cindy Crawford: These models contributed to the creation of an environment that allowed Lagerfeld to achieve his lofty goals by bringing their diverse family histories, social environments, and fresh fashion sense. The result was that he eventually made them so well-known that they could drop their last names. He managed to continually revitalize the brand with the help of Inès, Claudia, Cara, Kaia, and the rest of his girls without ever having to age himself.

4,765 square feet of living space was not excessive in Karl Lagerfeld's opinion. The living room featured three enormous arched windows that perfectly framed the view of the meandering Elbe River and the ships entering and leaving Hamburg harbor, as well as a gallery above the atrium that had plenty of room for bookcases. Karl was enthralled, according to Marietta Andreae, who was present for the initial viewing. He was curious about what it was like to return to his roots. Although it was intended to be a sort of homecoming, he ultimately chose to turn away from "back home."

The Blankenese home was a great concept. He spent his first year of life in Baurs Park, which was slightly over half a mile away as the crow flies. Additionally, it was situated on a slope with a view of the river, just like his earlier house. The villa also evoked his preferred era because it was constructed in the 1920s. The chance couldn't have come at a better time for Lagerfeld, who had lost his life partner, affectionately referred to as "Jako," two years prior and was now keen to dive headfirst into new endeavors. In 1991, he acquired the land and gave it the name Villa Jako.

Lagerfeld said goodbye to Marietta Andreae as he left for new opportunities. At Chanel, where she held the position of director of public relations for Germany and Austria until 2000, they had worked there for many years. Later, she moved on to concentrate on her own PR firm, but she kept working with Lagerfeld on numerous projects and photography exhibitions. Over the many years of their partnership, Andreae had witnessed the designer part ways with a number of close associates, so she was ready for what was to follow. In November 2007, everything just stopped. For Christmas, he sent her a huge basket filled with amaryllis and roses, but it was the last time.

Lagerfeld had left Hamburg, but he wouldn't remain there permanently. The following time Marietta Andreae saw him was on December 6, 2017 at the Elbphilharmonie. For his most recent Métiers d'Art exhibition, he was returning to his Hanseatic roots. When a reporter enquired as to whether the audience could anticipate seeing all the well-known Chanel fashion codes during the show, he responded, "This time they're my codes." He mentioned Hamburg as being a part of his own background. He described it as "wallpaper inside my brain."

The press and Karl Lagerfeld were great friends. The script is followed by other fashion designers, who have little to say about their designs and offer no general commentary. Designers who have established their own brands, like Jean Paul Gaultier, Christian Lacroix, Marc Jacobs, and Wolfgang Joop, are typically the only ones having a particular communication approach. But Lagerfeld was probably the only well-known designer with absolutely no social inhibitions among all the creatives who worked for large labels and could carry on a conversation. He would happily go on and express himself without regard for the businesses that were paying him.

Due to his friendship with the late WWD publisher John Fairchild and the then-editor-in-chief Patrick McCarthy, Lagerfeld was also a useful resource for Deeny and his successors Miles Socha and Jolle Diderich. Behind the scenes, the designer put a lot of effort into cultivating his media contacts. He got along well with German publishers Aenne and her son Hubert Burda (Elle, Bunte, Burda Moden, InStyle), as well as Samuel Irving ("Si") and his cousin Jonathan Newhouse from Condé Nast in New York (Vogue, GQ, Vanity Fair), Friede Springer from Springer (Bild and Welt newspapers), and Si. On November 10, 2005, in Offenburg, he attended Aenne Burda's funeral. In an almost inconceivable turn of events, he sprinkled some dirt over the casket in the grave and stated, "We have lost a great woman and a good friend."

Elizabeth Arden, a business partner of Lagerfeld's, hosted the product launch, and the cosmetics brand invited fashion editors from all over the world to attend. Over the ensuing decades, the custom of paying for journalists' travel, lodging, and pampering packages grew more prevalent. Major labels are now inviting editors to travel with them on multi-day excursions to places like Havana, Hamburg, Rio de Janeiro, Tokyo, Marrakech, and Palm Springs. Of course, these "destination shows" were all about the new mid-season collections, but they also gave the industry a much-needed lift. When it comes to spreading cheer, keeping key media figures happy, and enhancing editorial material, marketing spectacles like these are even more successful than a bouquet.

Francine Crescent, one of Lagerfeld's numerous pals, established the French edition of Vogue, the world's leading publication from 1968 to 1987 with her shamelessly provocative images. Her publication of Helmut Newton images, which "no other fashion magazine would have dared to print at that time," according to Karl Lagerfeld's 1982 essay, is noteworthy. He said, "She often risked her job" for him. In general, he was concerned with his interactions with the many editors-in-chief of Vogue over the years, notably Christiane Arp (Germany), Carine Roitfeld (France), Franca Sozzani (Italy), and Anna Wintour (US edition). He was constantly attempting to make friends with the fresh faces on the scene. He wasn't delighted when Roitfeld left French Vogue at the end of January 2011, but he was eager to get along with Emmanuelle Alt, who took over for her. Additionally, he regularly went out to dinner with Wintour on the first Sunday of Paris Fashion Week because, in his words, "the hours I spent with him at the table make me feel luckier than any stroke of luck I've had at my editing desk."

When the Bild tabloid published an article stating that Lagerfeld had ordered a crippled man to be ejected from first class on an aircraft in 1990, Lagerfeld felt so at ease with the media that he didn't even want to put up a fight. Matthias Prinz, his attorney, essentially had to persuade him to file a lawsuit. "So, is it true that something happened to a disabled man?" Prinz questioned him. I haven't taken a commercial flight in years, the designer simply answered. Prinz was granted compensation but was required to sign a non-disclosure agreement, therefore she has never disclosed the amount. On page one of Bild, an apology was printed.

In the controversy over the 1994 movie Prêt-à-Porter (which was released in the US as Ready to Wear), Prinz also represented Lagerfeld. One of the characters refers to Lagerfeld as a voleur, or a thief, in Robert Altman's parody of the fashion industry. Prinz explains, "He couldn't bear that. In March 1995, he was granted a temporary injunction that forbade the film's release in Germany as long as Lagerfeld was referred to as a thief, or Dieb in German. The movie studio came up with a brilliant workaround: they beeped over the offensive line. As a result, one of the fashion designers in the movie starts off by saying, "If I were Lacroix or that—beep—Lagerfeld... " In a Paris theater, Prinz saw the movie. It resembled the Rocky Horror Picture Show, where audience members would gather to applause and applaud during specific scenes.

At home, he received a lot of inspiration. Leo Tolstoy's War and Peace was his father's favorite novel, and he reproduced the images from it. Even though the vibrant pages of the periodicals his mother frequently brought back from Hamburg didn't offer him many opportunities at the time: He said as much in 2015. "I didn't yet know it was possible to make a career out of fashion," he added. I made the decision to create costumes for the theater as a result. Naturally, I later did that for the Scala and the Burgtheater as well. However, I don't have time for it anymore. Neither did he have any passion for it anymore. I'm not used to getting instructions. He was happiest when he was in charge of things. As in my movies. I direct and compose the dialogue, among other things. If not, I wouldn't be interested.

This type of nocturnal vision was described by Lagerfeld as an "electronic flash." And he made sure to keep a sketchpad near his bed in case he got an idea. If not, you simply forget it when you go back to sleep. He would put on a long, white smock shirt from Hilditch & Key first thing in the morning. "When you work with pastels and other colors, everything gets dirty." Everything else, including the shirts and bed linens, needed to be laundered daily. He remarked, "I prefer everything to be clean and white. "There is nothing I detest more than a stale stench. a messy bachelor? Thank you very much, but no. Once the nasty task is done, I shave and take a bath. So it is worthwhile.

Karl Lagerfeld's bookstore at 7 Rue de Lille served as the entrance to his literary universe. He would hover by the tables in his 7L store in the afternoon to see what was on exhibit before going into his photographic studio. Hervé Le Masson and Catherine Kujawski, his two booksellers, were constantly adding new titles to the collection. publications on everything from movies, theater, dance, crafts, gardening, and even a little bit of fashion were available, in addition to publications on photography, art, design, and architecture. He tapped the books and said, "Yes to this one, yes to that one, no to that one." With a 5 percent discount, Lagerfeld enjoyed this small luxury of purchasing his books from his own bookstore.

He was the best customer at other bookstores as well. He had been a regular at Galignani on Rue de Rivoli for years, and he claimed that his purchases there were responsible for 11% of the store's considerable sales. He frequented Rizzoli on Broadway in New York, the Bücherbogen in Berlin, Savignyplatz, and Felix Jud on the Neuer Wall shopping strip in Hamburg. He purchased one to twenty books a day for many years. He himself called his behavior "some kind of strange bulimia."

Since they used to place book reservations for him at La Hune on Boulevard Saint-Germain in the early 1980s, Lagerfeld had known both Hervé Le Masson and Catherine Kujawski. In 1999, he constructed his photography studio in the old courtyard on Rue de Lille, leaving a vacant front 860 square feet with big storefront windows facing the street. Le Masson received a lengthy letter from Lagerfeld when he was attending a training session in Nantes: "Would you be interested? Together, we could start a totally free and independent bookstore. On the Rue de Lille, they agreed to meet. Masson was led around the facility by Lagerfeld, who was photographing Carole Bouquet for Egoiste magazine in the studio that day. On December 7, 1999, they held an opening celebration for Iwao Yamawaki, a book about the Japanese photographer who had studied at the Bauhaus in Dessau from 1930 to 1932. It was the first book in Lagerfeld's recently launched 7L photo-book series, which he co-founded with his publisher, Gerhard Steidl.

Felix Jud on Neuer Wall in Hamburg was Lagerfeld's go-to bookstore in Germany. Wilfried Weber, whom Lagerfeld had met through Florentine Pabst in the 1980s, was the proprietor of the store. The two fell in love, and over time Lagerfeld emerged as Felix Jud's most devoted client. The employees would package the books and send them on to Paris after the designer had placed his orders through fax. Marina Krauth, a bookseller, took over taking care of Lagerfeld's bibliophile requirements after Weber passed away in 2016. She remembers that he had a wide range of interests. Johann Gottlieb Fichte, Friedrich Nietzsche, and Walter Benjamin were among the philosophers whose works he ordered, as well as complete editions of Thomas Mann's works and works by Joseph von Eichendorff, Hans Christian Andersen, and Rainer Maria Rilke. He purchased books on the Bauhaus movement, the history of the aristocracy from Metternich to Queen Louise of Prussia, and early film literature, including books on Fritz Lang's Metropolis and actresses Adele Sandrock, Asta Nielsen, and Eleonora Duse. He also purchased books on the architects Peter Behrens and Bruno Taut. Krauth claims that he was particularly attuned to the forerunners of graphic art, including illustrators like Henry van de Velde, Kay Nielsen, Léon Bakst, and Walter Schnackenberg. He also believed that women's art, particularly in relation to the Bauhaus, was truly revolutionary.

He was frequently more focused on the language, style, layout, structure, and paper than the actual subject. Not for the content, but for Proust's unique style, he was a fan. Coffee-table books on fashion, art, and design were his go-to purchases. Paper has a fragrance that no screen would ever be able to match, thus he had to be able to hold them in his hands. In a discussion about literature, he said to moderator Roger Willemsen, "I'm sorry, I adore iPads, but books are superior. "I want to flip through, touch the pages, and smell the paper." He shared this love of paper with Göttingen-based publisher Gerhard Steidl. Steidl is an authority on various types of paper and printing processes as a screen-printing specialist with his own internal printing division. Early in the 1990s, he dated Lagerfeld. He was once referred to by the designer as "the best printer in the world," and working with him encouraged the development of many fresh concepts. Starting with Off the Record in

1994, Lagerfeld collaborated with the publishing house to release dozens of photography compilations. In 2000, they came together to form L.S.D.

Lagerfeld could be very demanding of his friends because he reads so much. He was constantly recommending new books to Steidl, like the time he sent Reading Rilke: Reflections on the Problems of Translation by William H. Gass to Göttingen. Lagerfeld was extremely enthralled with the 1999 study. "You must read it," he commanded. It's really fascinating. He returned a week later and inquired, "Have you read it?" Steidl hesitated a while. The difficulties of translating Rilke's poems into English didn't pique his curiosity. Make the effort, Lagerfeld said. You must read it before we can discuss it, so please do. Steidl was compelled to admit that he had only read up to page thirty of the book when Lagerfeld called the following day. Lagerfeld became irate. Just remember this: I'd like to talk to you about literature if you read any of the books I recommend to you. We can just cancel everything if you don't want to do it. Steidl continued to read. He continued to read, and they collaborated once more.

Chapter 4:
The end time (2000 to 2019)

The millennium was the ideal opportunity to implement change. "Goodbye to my exquisite 18th-century furniture, which had been sold at auction. After ten years of devoted service, my Japanese clothing is leaving. The additional weight is gone. Hello, contemporary furnishings and clean-lined decor. Hello, peace of mind and problem-solving with composure. Lagerfeld concluded that, despite the potential long-term harm the excess weight could bring, "Vanity is good for one's health." He began a drastic diet on November 1 of 2000 and never looked back. Caroline Lebar explains, "He had made up his mind, and it was occurring. He eliminated everything that was negative for him and entirely transformed his relationship with eating. Lebar claims that the mere thought of sugar was enough to make him feel sick. And he had already shed ninety-two pounds in just thirteen months. He admitted to a German television host that "today my ambitions are bound to the superficial."

At the ideal time, Hedi Slimane's fashion revolution was beginning. When this young designer was hired by Bernard Arnault in 2000, he put the Dior menswear collection on a diet and came up with a slim silhouette that fundamentally changed the rules of menswear. As soon as he could fit into a size 48 at Dior, Lagerfeld was able to wear the jackets Slimane was creating. "As long as I can fit into a size 48 at Dior, then everything's fine." He soon changed into the same A.P.C. pants that his bodyguard Sébastien Jondeau was sporting, saying, "I wear the same size jeans as Sébastien!"

His attention to appearances has always been a top priority, even when he was considerably younger. He once jokingly said, "I think I was born wearing a tie." Like his hair, his ties continued to be a key component of his distinctive look. The other trends were all only fads. He chose the full beard style in the early 1970s: "I need over an hour to get it just how I want it," he once remarked. After washing and blow-drying his facial hair, his hairstylist at the Carita salon would shape it with a round brush, add some brilliantine for gloss, and end with a spritz of perfume. He used to cover his right eye with a rimless monocle, just like his mother did after the war. He was quite the dandy with his cravat, art deco accessories, and reinforced stand-up collar. Lagerfeld's longtime friend and German journalist Florentine Pabst rightfully referred to him as "the most immaculate luxury dandy in Paris."

He has a timeless design. He first thought of the ponytail in 1976 as a means of controlling his curly hair. His mother claimed that because of his bushy hair, he resembled "an old terrine" with its handle protruding. But I refrained from cutting it because it is commonly believed that doing so prevents it from growing back. He then decided on the most practical course of action: "All I have to do is brush it and wrap it in an elastic band, and it's done." Even while he was relaxing at home, he didn't let his hair down. Even when I'm sleeping, "I just tie the band lower so it's not so tight." He maintained the ponytail loose rather than pulling it back since he thought his hair was getting thinner as he aged. When it came to his fashion shows, hair played a significant role. "A full appearance consists of the girl, the clothing, the cosmetics, the hair, the shoes, and the accessories. Nothing is worse than working with cosmetics and hair artists who lack talent. I'd go crazy.

Over time, Lagerfeld's hairdo, known as his catogan in French, came to be recognized as his own. The use of white powder made the appearance much more distinguished and nearly presidential after the turn of the new millennium. "My mother's hair was originally pure white, but it ultimately turned black like the wings of a raven. My hair, which today would resemble an old cow's tail, was the color of Coca-Cola. His mother compared the color of his hair to "an old chest of drawers." The designer recalled seeing his mother's picture at a masquerade party. She had white hair in the picture, which was taken "around 1927," and he thought it was beautiful. "And my white hair is now powdered in the manner of the eighteenth century." It was a ritual: "Every morning I use dry shampoo to make it white, then I add a little lacquer to make it last. Then, in the evening, I give it another brush. He applied the dry shampoo in "a special powder room" because it was such a disaster and got all over the place. Only around once a month would his long-time hairdresser, who had been doing his hair for decades, visit him at home to wash his hair. "When I do it myself, I can't get my hair to dry properly—it gets curly after I wash it."

When it comes to fashion, Lagerfeld inherited his father's sense of style as well. Otto Lagerfeld made it a point to stop by Hilditch & Key, a bespoke shirtmaker, whenever he was in London or Paris. The Parisian location, which first welcomed customers on Rue de Rivoli in 1907, used to be a one-trick pony when it came to customized shirts. Since he was a teenager, Lagerfeld has done his shopping there. The company then began offering high-collar, wide-cuffed shirts at its stores in the middle of the 1970s. Lagerfeld created new collars and shirts as time went on for himself to wear. In order for Hilditch & Key to create the designs for him in a studio outside of Paris, he would give his chauffeur the sketches to leave at the store. Lagerfeld estimated that he ordered "more than three hundred different shapes and designs" of shirts from the company in total.

The majority of the shirts he purchased were polos made of Egyptian and sea island cotton. His smock shirts, which he wore when sketching, were another item that he had made to order. He was Hilditch & Key finest customer and frequently placed larger orders than the devoted politicians or managers who annually purchased forty or fifty customized shirts. The store was a go-to place for gifts as well. One of the beneficiaries was his friend at Chanel, Eric Pfrunder, to whom Lagerfeld gifted twenty shirts every year for his birthday. Due to all of his special orders, which occasionally included an additional forty cuffs or twenty collars, Lagerfeld went above the minimal price of about 700 euros ($850) for a tailored shirt.

His grandfather, the Prussian district administrator Carl Bahlmann, used to dress in a black-and-white style. It was amazingly adaptable as well. He might wear a white shirt and a black tie with a silver jacket or a black shirt and a white collar with an anthracite suit. On occasion, he would dress in all black with a pair of white pants for the summer on the Côte d'Azur. For big events, such as the fashion presentation in Havana in May 2016 when he made an entrance wearing a jacket covered in vibrant sequins (see p. 295), he could also dress it up. He largely adhered to the Chanel maxim, "One classic look, endless variations." In 2013, he declared, "You better change. You cannot compete or compare yourself to what you were before."

For this artist of self-styling, the monochromatic foundation served as a blank canvas on which he could add ties and jewelry to spruce up his appearance. He defied gender norms by choosing to accessorize with diamond lapel pins, brooches, or stone necklaces that are normally worn by women. In 2017, he decided to wear two tiny headphones hanging from a chain around his neck and a brooch by Suzanne Belperron featuring a photo of his cat Choupette. The earbuds were actually diamond-encrusted jewelry created by Nadine Ghosn, the daughter of Carlos Ghosn, the head of Nissan-Renault at the time.

When shaking hands, Lagerfeld donned fingerless gloves to protect his skin. He responded, "Because the world is nasty and polluted. He didn't have to take them off to shake hands with folks because they were fingerless. The gloves also helped cover up his mother's opinion that his fingers were overly fat and the age spots that were starting to appear on his hands' skin. He purchased them from the Chanel-owned glove manufacturer Causse (Gantier), which is located in Millau, close to Roquefort, the location of the renowned sheep's milk blue cheese. Numerous lambs are raised in the area, and Causse's products use the supple, lightweight leather from these animals. Each season, Lagerfeld placed orders with the French manufacturer for gloves made of eel or lamb leather, silver, gray, or black, and either studded or chained.

He opted to keep his hands mostly covered, but he wore Chrome Hearts rings every time. In the opening scene of the 2007 movie Lagerfeld Confidential, Lagerfeld takes a bowl and dumps all the rings he might possibly need for a quick trip to Monaco into a zipped bag, revealing the enormous size of his collection. It appeared as though he was making up for the shortcomings of the other males. Not to mention his mother's signet ring, he occasionally wore more than twenty rings at once. He also often wore the wedding bands of his parents around his neck on a necklace.

He was never truly alone, even when he was holed up in his flat at 17 Quai Voltaire, where he spent entire weekends whiling away the hours by himself. From the tourist boats traveling along the Seine below him, he would occasionally hear a loudspeaker announce, "Up there is where Karl Lagerfeld lives!" Gloria von Thurn und Taxis remembers a story he once related to her about a tourist who thought he had spotted him on the Quai. "That's Karl Lagerfeld," he affirmed. That couldn't be true, one of the others chimed in, "That's nonsense, he doesn't go out on the street anymore because of all the people."

However, there is a thin line separating a logo from a caricature. The year he died, Karl Lagerfeld was one of the most widely used inspirations for Halloween costumes. On October 31, 2019, thousands of copycats on Instagram proved the strength of his likeness by using the hashtag #Karl lagerfeld. The tradition continued during the "Grosses Têtes" at the Nice Carnival on February 15, 2020, when a gigantic Coco Chanel made an appearance driving a pram that contained a well-known face. In addition to sporting his signature high collar, black eyeglasses, and white ponytail, the larger-than-life Karl Lagerfeld also had a pacifier in his mouth. History is cyclical, but this time it's a joke rather than a tragedy.

Another quick choice was made by Karl Lagerfeld. Former French Vogue art director Donald Schneider ran a creative agency in Paris and frequently worked as a consultant for H&M. He developed the concept for a new advertising campaign for the Swedish apparel brand in 2014: blending high fashion with rapid fashion. A large name was required since it was a huge idea. He proposed that they try Karl Lagerfeld in a meeting with the brand. Would he even give it a thought? Schneider contacted him because he had to know. He questioned, "Karl, have you heard of H&M?" Of course!" There are also my assistants who shop," Lagerfeld retorted. What do you think about creating a little collection for them? Snyder inquired. Great concept! Future fashion will only consist of "high" and "low" styles; the remainder is already becoming boring. "Chanel has already taken care of the 'high' fashion," he remarked. A void therefore remained to be filled. "Wonderful. Then, we'll schedule a meeting," Schneider added. "Wait! Donald, one more query: "Did you consult with any other designers before coming to me?" Lagerfeld asked. "No, you're the first," Schneider retorted. That was sufficient for Lagerfeld to join the cause. "Okay, let's get started."

That is how everything started. It was a risky decision that required courage. Lagerfeld changed his mind after the collection had been created, the advertising campaign had long ago been completed in his studio on Rue de Lille, the billboards were up, and the retailers had received the deliveries. The night before the major unveiling in November, everything was ready to go, but Lagerfeld called Schneider in New York and said, "Donald, I can't get a wink of sleep. If it fails, what then? What if nobody shows up? Then, what will we do? "You'll see," Schneider promised him, "it will work." Even though he was aware of the Swedish company's strong marketing capabilities, he was uneasy. They were in uncharted territory because this was the pioneering effort of its type.

The collection's most affordable item was a T-shirt featuring a graphic design of Karl Lagerfeld that cost under 18 dollars (14.90 euros). Prior to Lagerfeld, the majority of consumers could hardly afford to purchase anything from a well-known fashion designer beyond lipstick or perfume. The collection, which included over 50 designs for both men and women, was sold in 500 H&M locations throughout Europe and North America. The items were more expensive than the rest of the line, although they were still far less expensive than high-end designer clothing. Naturally, Lagerfeld and his team were responsible for the clothing's design, but they also ensured its mass production and low production costs. In order to reflect Lagerfeld's unique style, the majority of the clothing was black, a color that is popular with both H&M's clientele and the designer himself.

Success for H&M was determined by the advantage the campaign gave them over rivals like Zara and C&A, as well as the additional revenue. Sales increased by 11% to 53.7 billion Swedish krona (more than 5 billion euros) in 2004. And the brand saw a 14 percent increase in sales in the fourth quarter after Lagerfeld's collection was unveiled. Officially, a new model of success was created. Elio Fiorucci, Stella McCartney, Viktor & Rolf, Roberto Cavalli, Lanvin, Versace, and other fashion designers created collections for the company after Lagerfeld set the example. Even brands who were previously only well-known to fashion connoisseurs, like Comme des Garçons, Marni, and Matthew Williamson, received their big break at H&M.

Lagerfeld became famous as a result of the partnership, but he wasn't content. Soon after the success story in 2004, he told Stern magazine, "They didn't produce large enough quantities, and the clothes were sold in less than half of the shops." I don't believe that's very polite of them, especially for individuals who reside in Eastern European countries and little towns. In what was supposed to be "anti-snobbery," he charged the corporation of being "snobbish." The limited-edition idea, which increased demand and made the garments harder to find, didn't convince him. Additionally, he believed that

H&M had increased the sizes of small clothing, which was unpopular.48 As time went on, Lagerfeld ceased criticizing the cooperation and began to praise it. Even though H&M had already moved on, he asked them about making another collection in the future. Along with collaborating with other designers, the business had also been successful in landing big-name celebrities like Madonna, Kylie Minogue, and David Beckham. The "Karl Lagerfeld for H&M" cooperation served as the template for all other partnerships that came after.

On June 5, 2008, they all attended the funeral service for Yves Saint Laurent at the Saint-Roch cathedral in Paris: President Nicolas Sarkozy and his wife Carla Bruni; designers Christian Lacroix, Sonia Rykiel, Valentino Garavani, Vivienne Westwood, and John Galliano; the mayor of Paris, Bertrand Delanoë; philosopher Bernard-Henri Lévy; actress Catherine Deneuve; model Claudia Schiffer; his old friend Victoire Doutreleau; his muse Loulou de la Falaise; and his mother, Lucienne Mathieu Saint Laurent, who passed away two years after him at the age of ninety-five. Everyone showed up to pay their respects to the designer, who passed away on June 1, 2008, from brain cancer. Karl Lagerfeld, an old friend of his, was the only one who stayed behind.

The 1970s left particularly severe scars. Around that time, Pierre Bergé was upset that the amour fou had made things more difficult with his partner and business partner, and Yves Saint Laurent was hurt that Jacques de Bascher had abandoned their relationship. Bergé ultimately decided to vacate the apartment on Rue de Babylone because their relationship was in such horrible form. On March 3, 1976, he checked into a room at the Hotel Plaza Athénée before relocating to an apartment on Rue Bonaparte.55 Lagerfeld's aggressive behavior, including openly accusing Bergé of being in love with Jacques himself, only fanned the flames. Through writer Alicia Drake, Bergé retaliated: "I do not fall into that trap," he declared. He then lost control of his temper and let his mouth run wild, so he did fall into a trap—just a different one.

The conflict had developed into something more. The two major designers were like magnets at the same pole, repelling one another.

"Lagerfeld never asked about Saint Laurent in my interviews," claims Godfrey Deeny. But he was curious about him in every way. In 1994, Joan Juliet Buck gave a reception in honor of being named editor-in-chief of French Vogue. Deeny later questioned Lagerfeld about the event after he had been invited to attend along with several other designers. He said, "I had one of the most repulsive experiences of my life." "Yves Saint Laurent approached me and gave me a cheek kiss. It needed to be washed off.

Pierre Bergé wrote his Lettres à Yves, some of which seem more like "Lettres à Karl " than letters to his late lover, as if to have the final say in the argument after Saint Laurent had died away. According to fashion historian Peter Kempe, Pierre Bergé despised Lagerfeld because he reprimanded him for being unimpressive. In the book, Bergé used the chance to push back, claiming that Coco Chanel and his late companion were the two most significant fashion icons of the 20th century: "Chanel in the first half, you in the second." With this arrogant attitude of entitlement—elevating Saint Laurent above even Christian Dior, the man who had paved the road for his career in fashion—he had, of course, every intention of upsetting Lagerfeld. Coco Chanel did mention that she might see Saint Laurent as her successor a few years before she passed away, but Bergé went so far as to suggest that he had to comfort her with a bouquet of flowers because Saint Laurent preferred to continue concentrating on his own design brand.

The departure of Saint Laurent from the fashion industry revitalized Lagerfeld. It was obvious that the clairvoyant had been accurate in her prediction that his opponent would blossom early and experience prominence in later years. He may ultimately emerge from his former friend's shadow over the ensuing seventeen years and steal the show. He changed with the times, responding well to the emergence of inexpensive fashion, the quickening of fashion cycles, the rise in the number of fashion shows, globalization, online marketing, social media, and haute couture.

Yes, the popularity of haute couture increased in the new millennium. The market was doing phenomenally well, with demand for custom clothing and tailoring soaring in emerging areas like

Russia, China, and the Middle East. A single piece of haute couture can cost more than $24,000 (20,000 euros), and some pieces can sell for more than 100,000 euros. But because the clothing is made with such high-end craftsmanship, these prices are acceptable. In reality, because the clothing is so expensive to create, businesses have minimal profit margins. The widespread use of the imagery of this timeless tailoring as a marketing strategy helps to increase sales of branded goods like fragrances and sunglasses.

For Lagerfeld, this was all incredibly fulfilling. Others were less fortunate: Christian Lacroix left Dior in 2011 after being forced to leave the company due to a drunken outburst in a bar, Jean Paul Gaultier abandoned couture in 2020, and John Galliano broke under the pressure in 2011. On the other side, Karl Lagerfeld was in complete control of everything, even himself. He persisted in the world of haute couture, demonstrating once more Pierre Bergé's errors. The Frenchman had asserted that ready-to-wear was favored by even affluent women in 1991, thereby declaring couture to be extinct. He added that Hubert de Givenchy and Yves Saint Laurent were the only remaining true couturiers. At the time, Lagerfeld referred to this somewhat ominous prognosis as "ridiculous". Finally, he had achieved victory. But it was a Pyrrhic victory because, even in the final years of his career, he was unable to create the kinds of timeless pieces of clothing that Yves Saint Laurent had.

When the ashes of the man dubbed "the last couturier" were spread in the rose garden of the Jardin Majorelle at Lagerfeld's estate in Marrakech on June 11, 2008, he was busy. The clairvoyant had told him, "It will begin for you when it ends for the others." He had just met Baptiste Giabiconi on June 8, 2008, which was an indication that the prophecy was about to be fulfilled. His final years were going to be incredibly fruitful.

The young French model was made famous by Lagerfeld in innumerable advertisements for brands like Chanel, Fendi, Hogan, and Dior. Additionally, he hired him for numerous fashion shoots and took pictures of him for numerous books. One of the very few guys to walk down the runway for the feminine brand Chanel is Baptiste. He was popular with the paparazzi even in 2008. Lagerfeld stayed in the villa he rented at La Réserve Ramatuelle throughout the summer holidays. Baptiste remained at position 16 with the designer, while Sébastien Jondeau and British model Jake Davies remained at position 19. At least when the three younger men weren't traveling to a nightclub in Saint-Tropez in the Lamborghini from his amazing fleet, Karl appreciated Baptiste's company when he wasn't working or reading. According to Gerhard Steidl, "They were young and liked to talk about new movies, new music, and the latest trends." They served as his point of contact with the outside world.

Karl also enjoyed getting his male friends to startle the paparazzi. He enjoyed having Sébastien drive him between Ramatuelle and Saint-Tropez because they could relax by the harbor, order a Pepsi Max, and let others stare. He would also be seen with Baptiste for the first time while strolling along the promenade in the summer of 2008. With his striking hairstyle, vibrant blouse, and little shorts, his new companion stuck out among the crowd. The media ate it up. A few days later, Karl and Baptiste enjoyed the results of their little stroll as they drove back to the waterfront in Karl's open-top Rolls-Royce. The media was enthralled by "la musa," the "friend of the summer," and Karl's "toy boy." Baptiste asserts that such newspaper coverage was crucial in "putting a planetary icon in a good mood." The fashion designer was about to begin "his greatest years"—his last and happiest reign as "Kaiser Karl."

Being so indispensable to this fashion god in his later years also became a burden for Lagerfeld. Caroline Lebar claimed that at the time, Lagerfeld had complete faith in his devoted bodyguard and driver. The Lagerfeld family called him "Seb," and he had to be present for Lagerfeld at all times. He lost his freedom of movement and even had to give up his favorite pastime, boxing. Lagerfeld couldn't stand it when he was away because he needed him to be at his beck and call. He controlled him and enquired after him. Every day, they discussed Lagerfeld's condition. With the same honesty the designer had always respected in him, Sébastien later remarked, "It was like a battlefield inside of me."

Lagerfeld was progressively losing strength. His stumbling on the runway could have been caused by his sciatica; he was receiving care from acupuncturist Nadia Volf as a result of years of sketching while sitting incorrectly. Additionally, he was learning to be more watchful after the incident where the carpet gathered and tripped him up at Chanel's famed mirrored staircase. After the Chanel haute couture show at the Grand Palais in July 2015, rumors about potential health issues began to spread. Models and celebrities like Kristen Stewart, Julianne Moore, and Rita Ora were seated at roulette tables in the palace, which had been turned into a casino for the occasion. Lagerfeld did not perform his customary lap of the runway this time, though. He didn't even walk far from the backstage area, just a few steps to the banister separating him from the audience. He never ventured farther than a short distance on the runway after that. In 2017, when the set had been converted into a waterfall, and again in 2018, when famous bouquiniste (bookseller) stands lined the catwalk, he briefly appeared at the conclusion of the presentation. The Vogue editor-in-chief Anna Wintour was in the audience, so he merely went forward briefly and nodded at her. Then he quickly vanished back into the wings.

In the very last seasons of his career, Lagerfeld began making appearances with his assistant Virginie Viard. She joined him for the first time on the bulwark of La Pausa, the replica ship named after Coco Chanel's home in Roquebrune-Cap-Martin on the Côte d'Azur, on May 3, 2018, during the Cruise show. On October 2, 2018, she joined him on the boardwalk at the man-made beach in the Grand Palais. The beach at Sylt was the setting for the beachside scene; he described it as the "least polluted place in the world" and "the beach of my childhood." He made the decision to go back in time for his last ready-to-wear show.

When he made his final runway performance at the Métiers d'Art show at New York's Metropolitan Museum in December 2018, his godson and assistant both held him by the hand. Being aware of his own mortality, he was already planning on Virginie Viard succeeding him. He referred to her as "my right and my left hand," and it was his way of saying "thank you" and "rewarding" her for her more than three decades of devoted work. It also enabled him to maintain his position as the most significant Chanel designer even after his death. There was a good chance that his legacy would be soon eclipsed if the fashion house hired a significant talent from outside the organization, like Nicolas Ghesquière or Hedi Slimane. Viard was named Lagerfeld's successor by the Wertheimer's barely hours after Lagerfeld passed away since they had no issue with his selection.

Lagerfeld started to steer clear of gatherings and events. When he went to the exclusive inauguration of a new Rimowa location on Rue du Faubourg Saint-Honoré in March 2017 and the private viewing of his own photography exhibition at the Palazzo Pitti in Florence in June 2016, he quickly left. Now, he just occasionally went out, and when he did, he was picky about where he went. He would only go to places he had been to before, like the Maison du Caviar, or he would only accept invites to private dinners, like those at Bernard Arnault's home. People who didn't regularly interact with him were more likely to notice his slow deterioration. When Baptiste Giabiconi asked Lagerfeld's buddy in 2016 why his face was bloated, Lagerfeld allegedly explained that he had been treated with cortisone for a persistent cold. When pressed, he acknowledged that the situation was more serious, that the American Hospital provided him with the best medical care, and that he had already undergone CT and MRI scans.

Later, during his later years, his failing health became more and more apparent. The faxes to Gerhard Steidl had shrunk from the customary fifteen or twenty pages to only two or three. His directions from 2015 weren't as exacting as they had been. He was also developing a pattern of sending Steidl his sketches later than planned.

The Metropolitan Museum's Métiers d'Art exhibition in New York City at the beginning of December 2018 was Lagerfeld's last significant trip. He then spent Christmas in Paris to prepare for the upcoming collections. Tuesday, January 22 had two haute couture shows planned: one at 10:30 am and another at 12 pm. Two days prior to the scheduled shows, Lagerfeld was checking in on the fit of the clothing, hair, and accessories at the fittings while seated in the studio with music expert Michel Gaubert, Chanel director Bruno Pavlovsky, and Chanel co-owner Alain Wertheimer. Suzy Menkes, a fashion journalist, released a brief Instagram video of Lagerfeld in which he appears oddly aloof. He is wearing spectacles without tinted lenses, as he has been doing recently, which makes it more clear that his eyes are sleepy. His eyes likewise appear tired. The same evening, Women's Wear Daily editor-in-chief Miles Socha observed Lagerfeld and noted that he appeared frail: "But because his mind was still sharp, you blocked out the fact that his body was getting weaker."

Despite being unwell, Lagerfeld never lost sight of the future. More ready-to-wear fashion presentations were anticipated, including those for Chanel and Fendi in early March. Mid-February, the designer was transported to the American Hospital. On February 13, he called Caroline Cnocquaert and placed a phone order for flowers: He responded, "No card," in a trembling voice. "You can write on the card." She had never experienced anything like this. She said to her spouse after hanging up, "It's all over." Then, while on the phone with her sister, she broke down in tears and said, "Stéphanie, he's not going to be with us for much longer." He last placed orders for bouquets for Caroline of Monaco, Bernard Arnault, and an old friend who plans private parties, Françoise Dumas.

Sébastien Jondeau held Karl Lagerfeld's hand as he died at 10:20 a.m. on February 19, 2019.161 Baptiste Giabiconi was one of the first individuals Sébastien called. "It has left. He said, "It's over; he's left. It's done.

The renowned decoration given to Karl Lagerfeld by President Nicolas Sarkozy in 2010—the highest civil honor bestowed by France—is noted on his death certificate as a Commander of the Legion of Honour. His penthouse residence in the Millefiori complex, located at "1, allée des Genêts, Monaco," is listed as the address on the certificate. The certificate was granted at 11:06 a.m. and was signed by the registrar, Anne-Marie Foubert, so everything was processed promptly. The French news agency AFP's German affiliate then reported: "Fashion designer Karl Lagerfeld: dead at 85." The "official statement from Paris regarding the passing of Mr. Lagerfeld" and the choice of Virginie Viard as his replacement was released by Chanel's German press office two minutes later, at 1:07 p.m.

Most of the other news headlines at the time were overshadowed by the media coverage of Lagerfeld's passing. Only significant political events and global happenings garnered more attention than the passing of this German in Paris, including the election of Boris Johnson as British prime minister and the uncertainty surrounding Brexit, Greta Thunberg's public appearances and the climate crisis, US President Donald Trump and his many detractors, the European elections on May 24, the appointment of Ursula von der Leyen as the new President of the European Commission, the Hong Kong protests, the Syrian war, and the fir In 2019, a number of notable people passed away, including Jacques Chirac, Peter Lindbergh, Hannelore Elsner, Doris Day, Niki Lauda, Toni Morrison, Peter Fonda, Ferdinand Pich, and Robert Mugabe. But none of these passages brought forth such a global flood of remembrances, obituaries, TV specials, and special editions.

The most understated tribute of them took place on German television that very evening. Claus Kleber, the host of the news programm Heute Journal, started the show at 9:45 p.m. wearing a gray suit, a white shirt, and a burgundy tie with white spots. However, Kleber was donning a black tie in honor of the fashion designer when Gundula Gause finished reading the news and the camera turned back to him. Of course, the death notice for Karl Lagerfeld was the final piece of news for the day.

Everywhere in the world, people were in grief. According to President Emmanuel Macron, fashion had lost "its most famous ambassador." Melania Trump, the first lady, referred to Lagerfeld as "a creative genius." However, Germany's top decision-makers kept silent. After all of Lagerfeld's criticism of her, Chancellor Angela Merkel may have felt no duty to laud him. But Federal President Frank-Walter Steinmeier remained nothing, despite the fact that only a few days earlier, he had complimented the late Swiss actor Bruno Ganz for representing "the highest highs and the lowest lows of German history." Peter Tschentscher, the first mayor of Hamburg, did have something to say about the late designer, describing him as "an extraordinary Hanseatic citizen and ambassador of Hamburg." According to Michael Roth, Minister of State for Europe at the German Federal Foreign Office, the late Mr. Lagerfeld had "probably done more for German-French relationships than many politicians."

The Milan Fendi show went on as scheduled two days following Lagerfeld's passing. David Bowie's "Heroes" and Lou Reed and John Cale's "Smalltown," which is about a child from a tiny town who wants to leave and find his place in the world, were two of Michel Gaubert's music selections for the performance. The audience applauded Silvia Fendi when she entered the runway by herself to make her bow. The exhibition came to a finale with a film shot in 2013 showing Karl Lagerfeld drawing himself as he appeared on his first day at Fendi in 1965, down to the last Cerruti hat and Scottish tweed Norfolk jacket.

The funeral for Lagerfeld was held in the Paris neighborhood of Nanterre the next day, and those closest to him were there. Along with her daughter Charlotte and son Andrea Casiraghi, Caroline of Monaco attended. Along with his wife Hélène Mercier, kids Antoine and Alexandre, Bernard Arnault arrived. Gerhard Steidl, Inès de la Fressange, and Anna Wintour were all present. Alain and Gérard Wertheimer, Virginie Viard, Bruno Pavlovsky, and Eric Pfrunder were Chanel's representatives. Then there was Karl's fictitious family, which consisted of Brad Kroenig, his wife Nicole, and their boys Hudson and Jameson, as well as Sébastien Jondeau, Caroline Lebar, Pier Paolo Righi, Choupette and her maid Françoise Caçote. There were also his devoted seamstresses, led by debutante Anita Briey, who had worked with the designer for more than 50 years, beginning with his early days at Chloé.

The ceremony was not presided over by a cleric. Even Thoma Schulenburg, the daughter of Lagerfeld's half-sister Thea, and Christel's daughter and two sons who reside in the US were not invited. It was a covert meeting. Nevertheless, when the hearse bringing the black coffin to the Crématorium du Mont-Valérien drove by, there were between sixty and eighty people standing along the roadside.

Funerals made Karl Lagerfeld angry. He jokingly quipped that there wouldn't be a funeral when the time came for him to pass away. I'd rather go away.166 The designer requested that his ashes be combined with those of his mother and Jacques de Bascher before he went away. Sébastien Jondeau was given the job of making him vanish without a trace. A few days following the cremation, he dispersed or buried the cremated remains someplace in France. True to his pledge, he kept everyone in the dark about the location and method of his deed. There is no monument in place.

The fashion legacy of Lagerfeld was assured. His work ethic has been imitated by other designers, and his example has encouraged many more to pursue careers in design. Not only that, but Virginie Viard, the candidate he had favored, immediately took his place at Chanel. The most significant fashion house in France was once again led by a woman, over 50 years after the death of Coco Chanel in 1971. In the year after his passing, other collections continued to carry on Lagerfeld's legacy. At the fashion presentations in February and March, jackets with Chanel-inspired styling could be seen everywhere, including Marc Jacobs, Donatella Versace, Hedi Slimane (Céline), and Alessandro Michele (Gucci). Bridget Foley, a fashion journalist, called it "the best kind of homage."167 There was one last remembrance to the late designer. The Karl Lagerfeld Prize replaced the LVMH Prize for Young Designers in the summer of 2019. The inaugural recipient of this new prize was the gifted young Israeli Hed Mayner, who also received a mentorship program and 150,000 euros. Due to the fact that his career had also started after receiving a fashion award, Lagerfeld felt faith in the LVMH Prize.

It was time for the Chanel ready-to-wear show, which would serve as Lagerfeld's final message to the world, on March 5, two weeks after his passing.168 In a black Chanel jacket, Lars Eidinger left the house. It was initially intended for women, but when worn by a male, it gave him a peculiar aura of reversed liberty that was both traditional and laid-back. Due to the four patch pockets, Coco Chanel based her renowned tweed suit on men's tailoring. And then here came this German actor who was blurring the gender roles in the other way. Lagerfeld was described by him as "insanely free and downright anarchic."

A bell chimed to signal the start of the play, almost like a church service. Oversized skirts, suits, caps, and coats. Flat, stitched, diamond quilted bags with the recognizable interlocking CC clasp. Karl Lagerfeld and Virginie Viard's design for the new Chanel "19" bag was both a message for future generations and a timeless classic like the "2.55." The Chanel "19" is named after the year it was introduced, and like the Chanel No. 19 perfume, it alludes to Coco Chanel's birthdate of August 19, 1883. Of course, they were unaware of the upcoming year (2019) or day (February 19) of Lagerfeld's passing when they came up with the moniker for this new bag.

The tolling of the bells, the moment of silence, the devotion: Lars Eidinger described it as being "very spiritual." Karl Lagerfeld "tells us what it is like to die, and he does it with a sense of humor," the man said, describing the fashion presentation as seeming like a secular liturgy. The last models were dressed in spherical "snowball dresses." Penélope Cruz or Kaia Gerber will likely come to mind when people think back on this collection. They will appear to be floating through the glass palace like cotton balls. Finale of a fashion creation tale: Concepts became reality, plans were put into action, and time stood still. The models' footprints in the fake snow were concealed by the enormous capes. That is how Karl Lagerfeld wished to go as well—completely unnoticed. And that's exactly what he did the morning of the Chanel show.

Printed in Great Britain
by Amazon

41401216R00066